"George Mullins is one of the best exam
book is a treasure of military history to be enjoyed by
tary experience and others who just enjoy reading a good story."—Gary
L. Brown, Brigadier General, U.S. Army (Retired)

"Foxhole is a captivating read. George Mullins' true experiences during
WWII are described in such amazing detail that you literally feel you
are there with him. You experience his anxiety and distress as he accepts
the realities of war, while sharing his journey toward emotional and
spiritual peace. If you are only going to read one book this year, this is
the one." —Carolyn Fox, author of Soul Rider: Facing Fear
and Finding Redemption on a Harley

"George Mullins has given us an authentic, first-person account of his
personal odyssey with the 101st Airborne Division during World War II.
From Normandy to Holland, to Bastogne, and on to Berchtesgaden, he
saw it all. A country boy from Virginia who was swept up into an epic
war with a famous unit, he recounts the suffering and sorrow of war but
seasons it with his endearing, humorous observations. Men like Mullins
are the reason Tom Brokaw coined the phrase "Greatest Generation." It's
an honor to call George my friend." —Dan Herbster, Former Division Historian for the 101st Airborne Division (Air Assault)

"Foxhole is a must read. If you ever wondered what it was like for the
men who took up arms to defend freedom and change the course of the
world, look no further. George's stories, descriptions, and depictions
paint the picture of what life was like going through WWII. You'll laugh,
be amazed, and most of all, feel proud of what was accomplished, it's
nothing short of heroic, and Foxhole confirms the definition that we all
use to describe these great men...America's greatest generation."
—Kathryn Edwards, Director at Best Defense Foundation

FOXHOLE

George K. Mullins

Memoir
BOOKS
Chico, CA

Published by Memoir Books
An Imprint of Heidelberg Graphics

Library of Congress Control number: 2021939687

Ordering Information:
For details, contact foxhole@asis.com.

ISBN 978-1-937748-38-8 paperback

Cover Artwork by Karen Bauer
Layout and Design by Jay Biancalana

Printed in the United States of America.

Preface

I started writing this book seventy-three years after I first set foot on the beaches of Normandy, France. I have always felt that my part in World War II was nothing more than a needle in a haystack. My intention was to write a book about my personal experiences during the war. I have tried to tell my story with no prejudice; just the facts as I remember and have observed. It is my story. It is a journey and adventure as well as an education in what the war was like for a young, eighteen-year-old farm boy from Virginia. It is dedicated to all the gallant men and women who weren't as fortunate as me; those that never made it back home, including the men who died in Operation Tiger, and the mothers, fathers, friends, relatives, and especially, the children who had to bear the tragedy and grief of never seeing their loved ones again. It is an honor to have known and served beside these heroes.

Acknowledgments

There are so many people I would like to thank who have helped me make this book a reality. I could write another book just to thank each and every one of you. You are all loved for your support. A big shout out to the Screaming Eagles, my brothers in arms, who have shared my experiences. Many thanks to my family and friends for their support over the past 74 years as I worked my way through all the demons and experiences of the war. Your patience is greatly appreciated. My wonderful family has stood beside me through thick and thin. I would also like to thank everyone who took the time to read my story and provide feedback to me, helping me write the best book I could.

I want to give special thanks to the following people: Ms. Karen Bauer for her poems and for being a dear friend; Peter Plank and his wife, Linda, for their company and friendship over the years, as well as representing The Liberty Jump Team; my friend, Denis Van Den Brink, for his unbelievable support while writing this book; author Kevin Brooks for the many discussions and information about the timeline of my story. My warmest regards and deep appreciation go to Kathryn and Donnie Edwards of The Best Defense Foundation. Through your work, I have been blessed to return to many of the places where I fought and special places like the Eagles Nest, sharing memories along the way. I will carry these experiences with me the rest of my life. Much love to my sister, Dicie, for all her work organizing our trip to Europe in 2017, where I received the French Legion of Honor and the keys to the city of Carentan. She also put me in contact with the Best Defense Foundation. Thank you also to Anne Lyse and Peter Johnson, owners of the Kyraid Hotel and Restaurant in Carentan, France, for providing me with a nice bed, excellent food, and great conversation on a number of my trips to Europe. I am most grateful and humbled by the gift of the friendships I have made in my travels back to Europe. There are so many people that have become like family to me.

Many thanks to my daughter, Sheila Maraigh, for taking the time to diligently edit my story for me. And last but not least, I want to express my gratitude to my friend and partner in many adventures, Jay Biancalana, for spending the time with me and helping me get my story out of the stars and onto paper. Without his experience and understanding of military life, this book might not have been written.

Kay Martin was my first real love. Most men only find true love once in a lifetime. It only took me fifty years, but I was blessed with finding another person who really taught me about true love: my loving wife of forty years, Lucila. She was and will always be the light of my life. Thanks to all my children and grandchildren for always loving and tolerating me throughout the years. I am a better man because of all of you. Finally, my biggest thanks go to the people of the war-torn European countries. Your bravery and support both during and after the war is an example to all humankind.

Foxhole: a hole in the ground used by troops
as a shelter against enemy fire or as a firing point.

Ode to the Stars

Huddled in my foxhole
A few feet deep
So cold and so tired
Unable to sleep

I gaze up to you
A comforting sight
Your twinkle offers hope
And reminds me there is light

In this darkness, this void
This human disgrace
You remind me of home
That faraway place

I gaze up to you
For a moment it is still
You must have plan for me
If I have the will

The will to believe
To trust in your plan
You guided me as a boy
Please protect me as a man

Some nights I search for you
When it's too smoky to see
I admit I am relieved
That you can't look upon me

Amidst the mess and the horrors
That occur in the night
When men lose their way
When men lose their light

But tonight it is clear
You shine bright in the sky
Your radiance reflected
In every lonely man's eye

We are the fortunate
The ones still alive
Left to carry your light
Carry on and survive

You must have a plan for me
If I have the will
I give you my trust
For a moment it is still

In this stillness, it is safe
Safe to let my heart roam
To dream of that place
The place I call home

Huddled in my foxhole
A few feet deep
I feel a bit calmer
I will try now to sleep.

Karen Bauer ©2019

Table Of Contents

Chapter 1
Introduction

Young George
1933

    On April 29, 1925, Bill (William) and Minnie (Mintie) Mullins of Jenkins, Kentucky, welcomed the arrival of their second son, George Kenis Mullins. This is my story. I had six brothers and four sisters before our family was finished. My dad spent a big part of his life in the coal mine. I remember him telling me he saw daylight only one day a week, Sunday, his sunshine day. He and the other miners used carbide lights to see inside the dark dungeon called the coal mine. They had no safety equipment. No helmets to protect their heads from injury or respirators to protect their lungs. Breathing all that soot and dust would eventually lead to black lung disease, but they didn't really have a choice. The miners all knew the risks, but they also knew they needed the money. Like most coal miners, my father entered the mine before daybreak and returned well after dark. If he didn't work hard, we wouldn't survive.

Miner's cap.
Courtesy of the Division of Work and Industry, National Museum of American History, Smithsonian Institution.

Miner's pick and shovel.

1

With only a pick and a coal shovel, he would load a full ton of coal, receiving a dime for all his labor.

About 1930, Dad bought acreage in the Cumberland Mountains, twelve miles southeast of the tiny community of Pound, Virginia, where, with much needed help, he built a three-room cabin. My dad was capable of many things, but he was no carpenter. I am thankful for the people who lent a hand.

After the cabin was built, my dad got very ill and couldn't work. Not only did Mom have to take care of the house, children, and her regular chores, but until he recovered, she had to take care of Dad as well. She did what she had to do for all of us to survive. As always, she planted and tended the garden, canned its bounty, foraged food from the wild, milked the cows, cared for the chickens, and made most, if not all our clothes. Mom did it all. Throughout each day, she would only take breaks to come into the house to make one of the three meals of the day. She was the first one up and the last one to bed each day. Never once did I hear her complain. Through thick and thin, she was always there and always had time for me and my siblings.

As soon as I was old enough, I began helping her as much as I could. She never asked, it was just the right thing to do. With minimal education, my mom was one of the smartest people I have ever known. I am fortunate that she passed on much of her knowledge to me. Spending time with her was not only educational, but it also established a bond between her and I that could never be broken. I know she loved all her children, but I think, because I almost died as a baby, she had a special connection to me and I to her. To this day I value the lessons she taught me.

I can remember at the beginning of the Great Depression when my mom, Grandma, and I would walk thirteen miles and back in a day to get our monthly handful of government rations. Twenty-six miles in a day! I was only about six or seven, but like the rest of my family, I was ever grateful for what little we received. The people living in the rural areas at this time are living a pioneer lifestyle. The depression requires most folks outside the city to live off the land, as there are few jobs and very little money. I am fortunate to have a background in this type of living. We survive without going to the store to purchase anything except flour, salt, and baking powder. Dad does everything he can to keep us fed. He produces his own sugar or as close to it as he can. He grows his own sugar cane and processes it down to molasses using a two-roller mill to extract the sweet liquid from the cane stalks. It has an engine that runs on four steel shoes. We call her Nell. She is quite a special horse.

We live off the land and the food we hunt, plant, and grow. We have no electricity or indoor plumbing, only an

Dad and Nell converting sugar cane into molasses with a two-roller mill.

outdoor outhouse. At this time in history, it seems the whole United States is in some sort of chaos- from the East Coast, to the plains of North Dakota, Nebraska, the deserts of New Mexico and all over the country. Fortunately, pioneer living is the way of life for most of the people around me. In many ways, it is actually a better lifestyle than the lifestyles that folks who live in the cities experience. For those who live in one of the larger cities, things seemed much worse in so many ways. Trying to plant and raise a garden in asphalt and concrete instead of fertile soil yields next to nothing. They have little or no opportunity to hunt, fish, or raise food for themselves. For them, it is only the soup lines, and sadly, many don't make it through the line to ever get their soup bowl filled.

In 1932, the United States elects a new president. His name is Franklin D.

Schoolchildren line up for free issue of soup and a slice of bread during the Great Depression.

Roosevelt. He is a survivor of polio. Once elected to office, one of the first things he does is act swiftly to stabilize the economy and provide jobs. He has the government provide relief to those who are in need. He creates "The New Deal." The New Deal is a series of programs and projects instituted with the intent of helping Americans get out of poverty. He also starts an organization known as the CCC (Civil Conservation Corps). The CCC provided millions of young men with employment on environmental projects. He signs into law the WPA (Works Progress Administration) to carry out public works projects, including the construction of public buildings and roads. He gives the people the right to form a union, bringing safety and higher wages to the workplace. He creates the Social Security Administration so workers will have savings when they become old. At a time when people are hungry, they receive food from the government, preventing them from starving.

To grow up during the depression isn't all that bad through the eyes of a young boy in Virginia. To me, it is just a normal way of being. All the children around me live the same as

President Roosevelt in his wheelchair with Ruthie Bie and Fala. February 1941. Photo courtesy of FDR Presidential Library & Museum. Photograph by Margaret Suckley.

4

Children worked in both the coal mines and in the factories until 1938 when child labor laws came into effect. These children were oyster shuckers in Mississippi. https://www. goodfreephotos.com

me. I work right alongside the adults at home on the farm. If you don't work, you don't eat. Thankfully, I do not have to work in the coal mines or industrial factories to survive as many young children in the United States do. This doesn't change until 1938 when child labor laws come into effect. Most of us just try to help one another. Survival is difficult, but to me, that seems normal, no one is any better off than anyone else.

We have four seasons: spring, summer, fall, and winter. In the spring, everything begins to come back to life. As the crops get planted, the sound of bird songs fills the air, and the trees begin to bloom. Summer months are hot and humid. The fall is the most beautiful of all as the different trees begin to change color, dropping leaves, their vivid shades of red and gold, contrasting against the kaleidoscope of the season's colors as winter nears. This is the time of year I am most excited. For me, hunting and trapping is the way I can make some money to help me and my family. If I fail to catch enough mink, I won't make enough money to afford the boots I need, and I will go barefoot through the winter. Also, a cottontail rabbit is a prize dish, especially during the cold winter months. The winter months will bring the frosty, cold temperatures in before the first snow. The snow can get as deep as four feet at the height of the season. My brothers and I run and slide off the hills on our homemade sleighs, at least until the snow gets too deep.

I am about twelve or thirteen when a man from New York shows up. His name is Mr. Dibble. He is going to be our Sunday school teacher. I hear a rumor about Mr. Dibble. When he, along with his wife and children, moved down to Virginia from New York, he stopped at a gas station. The attendant filling his gas tank asked Mr. Dibble, "Where are you going?" Mr. Dibble replied, "I came down from New York to save the heathens." I think he is more of a heathen than a holy man because he ends up making this place his home and chooses to live in our community.

Mr. Dibble had a sidekick at Sunday school. I think his name was Mr. Foster. It was a long time ago, but I do remember he was exceptionally tall and lanky or at least to me he was. One day, Mr. Foster came to visit my family while I was out trapping. When I came home, I walked in carrying a grain sack loaded with a fiery red fox with an injured paw. This fox was as mad as a hornet, and I knew it, but Mr. Foster, with his naive New York education, knew nothing of wild animals and the danger

My parents, Bill and Minnie Mullins.

My grandparents, George and Nancy Church, with my Aunt Berdie and my Uncle Leonard. This is the log cabin where Grandpa put a sulphur match head into the wall when I learned to shoot.

they can present, especially when wounded. He just absolutely had to have this fox. He says to me, "I'll give you FIVE dollars for that fox." Now, I'm just a simple country boy, but I know what five dollars means to me and my family. I try to explain to Mr. Foster he really doesn't want this fox, but he absolutely must have this fox! He hands me the five dollars and is on his way without any incident. Arriving home, he can't wait to show his wife this lovely creature he just bought for a beautiful pet. This beautiful animal nails his sharp teeth through Mr. Foster's hand, resulting in one of the nastiest infections. He decides afterward that a fox doesn't make a great pet and he has the fox's pelt made into a beautiful stole for his wife.

I love growing up at home. My parents are great role models. My grandparents live only a couple of miles away, and they are quite active in my rearing and education. I stay with them every chance I get. My grandpa had very little education but a lot of common sense and all the life skills a boy could ever desire. He shows me how to do so many different things. He knows all the good, safe local foods and herbs to eat and where to find them. He teaches me to be a fisherman, hunter, trapper, and an expert rifleman. He uses a sulphur match head stuck into a bullet hole that is in an old log as the target when he teaches me to shoot. He shows me how to farm and tend to the livestock at home, but mostly, he teaches me how to face the world and use my common sense. In his younger days, he made it a point never to let moonshine go to waste. I am forever thankful to him. I know I will carry my grandpa's lessons and outlook all the days of my life.

Like all young farm boys at the time, I have numerous chores I must do each morning when I get up. The livestock needs tending and firewood must be restocked before I have breakfast and get ready for school. My day really gets started after I finish my chores. That's when I gather my books and walk to the grade school which is two miles away. When I get older, I walk four miles to the high school. As a teenager, my schooling becomes more sporadic. Harvest time is a huge interruption to my schooling, as well as to most children I know. I am taken out of school for at least a month each year to help with harvesting the crops. The harvest must be done by any means if we are to survive through the winter.

When I was a teenager, the South Fork of the Pound River froze solid one winter. My school friends and I decided to go ice skating on our way to high school. I am having a great time, right up until I take a terrible fall, knocking myself unconscious. The boys with me spend a few minutes

Flat Gap High School where I attended school. This school was all hand built thanks to the WPA. My granddad helped build this school. Each stone was hand-split, and all the concrete was hand mixed and poured. Now listed in the National Register of Historic Places, it is currently a community center.

8

getting me awake and back on my feet, but I have to walk three more miles before I get to the school. I was completely disoriented. Most likely I suffered a concussion. I should have told my parents or seen a doctor, but there was no doctor close by and my parents weren't really going to be able to do anything. I walk about a mile before my head begins to clear. I am having a hard time seeing, and it takes some time to finish my journey. I don't remember much of that hour. I had been carrying my lunch sack the whole time and never realized it. The rest of the year my grades really show the damage done by that fall. In fact, when I entered military service, I continued having problems from that concussion.

As a teenager, I find I am very interested in the current events of the world. I am so fortunate my family owns a battery-powered radio. I pay special attention when news about the ruler of Germany, Adolph Hitler, is mentioned. As a young teen, my mind creates this vision that he and his Nazi regime are like a tornado moving across Europe, as fast as lightning, destroying human life and causing more extreme suffering than the world has ever known. Most of the countries of Europe are overrun by the Nazi regime. Hitler has plans, especially for the British. He made it clear that rejection of his appeal to "reason" would result in a "final" attack upon Britain with every resource that Germany could throw into the battle. He launches an attack called "the Blitz." The Blitz is a German bombing offensive against Britain.

From September 1940 to May 1941, Hitler and his Nazi regime bombed the British continually, day and night, causing enormous destruction and heavy civilian casualties; some 43,000 civilians were killed and another 139,000 were wounded. Surprisingly, instead of surrendering, the nonstop attacks only made the British angrier. In the city of London, the train system goes below ground. They don't use coal burners down below, only electric cars. Fortunately, when the system was designed, it was designed deep enough into the ground that no bombs have ever penetrated it. This makes for an excellent place for people to go during bombings who don't have access to an air raid shelter. At the height of the Blitz and probably throughout the war, many British people lived or spent time down in this railway system, especially at night, when the German bombing was most active. I am certain that many lives were saved because of the train system below the ground.

British citizens living in the railway system during the Blitz. Courtesy of the National Archives, photo no. 195768.

After Japan's Pearl Harbor attack on December 7, 1941, the United States enters World War II and comes to the defense of its original mother country, England, before Germany kills the last Englishman on earth. I am only sixteen, too young to join the military. I hear of so many young men from all over the United States who are joining the different branches of military. Time passes quickly, and as I turn seventeen, I find myself frustrated that I am again falling behind in my schooling. I really want to finish high school, but with being taken out of school each year for the past few years, I need more time than I feel I have. I have already made up my mind to join the military after I finish school, but my plans change, and I leave school without graduating. I turn eighteen, and a couple of months later, I sign up for the draft. I am offered a place in the Navy. Thanks, but no, that's not for me. I pick the Army; it feels like a much better fit. On September 30, 1943, I am officially inducted into the Army.

As I prepare to leave home, I don't realize how this new life will teach me about the bigger world. I also discover that even in the worst fighting, knowing how to field dress a pig to make chops will earn me the gratitude of many fine, young city boys.

Chapter 2
Camp Wheeler, Georgia

Camp Wheeler, Georgia, 1943.

On October 21, 1943, I say my goodbyes to my family and board a bus to Abington, Virginia. I, along with Edward Shortt and Julius Meade, two young men I am friends with from Pound, Virginia, get our physicals and immediately after board a train going to Camp Wheeler, Georgia. I never thought that a young, inexperienced boy from the hills would be boarding a train for the first time on his way to Camp Wheeler, Georgia. One might think my mind would be filled with the adventures that lie ahead in the army, but instead, I'm more concerned with how fast this train goes. This is my first of many train rides I'll be taking, and let me tell you, it does not live up to my expectations. The ride is slower than molasses. Maybe I'm a fast-minded guy, but I've seen cows move faster than this train.

Old coal-burning locomotive.

This old coal-burning train is from another time. It rumbles and shakes non-stop, clickety-clickety-clack, as it passes over each joint of the tracks. Imagine trying to sleep in a box being shaken and banged on the ground. That is my ride. I finally arrive at Camp Wheeler mid-afternoon the next day. My mind is overwhelmed with the change of scenery as well as the changes army life introduces. Talk about a different world! There are so many different nationalities and dialects of speech. Young guys from all over the country with their unique mannerisms and attitudes, and here I am, just a country boy from the mountains between Virginia and Kentucky who has never been around anyone outside of my small world. I find it most interesting, but I am also a bit intimidated and wary. After we get processed, including haircut and uniforms, it's almost impossible for me to recognize any of these men, including my two friends, Shortt and Meade. I am lucky I have them to go through basic training with me. It appears to me that many of these men have extremely bad attitudes and are not shy about letting everyone else know how they feel about their current situation. Talk about waking up on the wrong side of the bed!

The next seventeen weeks of my life will transform me from a civilian to a soldier in the United States Army. As I begin to adjust to my new environment and way of life, I must learn to adapt and get along with all these different men, especially the homesick ones. The homesick recruits really get to me. I, too, am a little homesick myself, but their attitudes and negativity make me a bit angry and apprehensive around them. There is one incident I remember well. A bad-attitude coal miner stepped up to me during training and says, "I'll take you out of ranks!" I'm a little surprised, as I haven't said a word to this man. He says, "I'll take you out to the parade grounds and teach you a lesson." I'm keeping really quiet, but after a little while, my blood has reached my brain, and I'm seeing red. Noon comes and we return to the barracks. I walk over to this guy and say, "I'm ready, let's go to the parade grounds." He wastes no time and punches me in the face. I've always been one to try and get along, and although I have had my experiences with the school bullies before, this guy hitting me is like lighting a short fuse on a big stick of dynamite. I get hold of him and immediately start pummeling him.

I black both his eyes in my rage, not even knowing or caring. This is abruptly ended by the rest of the recruits in the barracks. It takes most of the platoon to get us separated. A short time passes, and my attacker and I are called in to speak with the barracks NCO (Non-Commissioned Officer in Charge). He looks at the two of us and says, "You guys shake hands. You're on the same team, so act like it." This is my first lesson in teamwork. We shake hands, but it's my nature to be uneasy around others and a loner. It's going to take a long time for me to trust others and to feel as if I am a part of this new family.

Our training regime crowds a lot of education into our brains and bodies within a short period of time. There are few day passes to town, no furloughs, no in-house visits, no signs of any love or compassion, and no nonsense. We eat, drink, and sleep the "army way." If you don't know what that means, you learn really fast. There is a right way, a wrong way, and the "army way," which usually yields the same results as the wrong way but takes much longer. It seems as if training is nonstop. We do a lot of calisthenics and marching in formation, but mostly, we are learning to work together as a team. We have hours of training for each of the various weapons. Light weapons training covers many weapons, including the military-issued rifle, the M1 Garand, the air-cooled .30 caliber

M1 Garand with bayonet.

.30 caliber air cooled machine gun and tripod, with 250 round belt.

Browning Automatic Rifle (BAR) with 20 round clip and tripod.

machine gun, and the fast-firing BAR, (Browning Automatic Rifle.) And let's not forget the bazooka, grenade, and 60-millimeter mortar. It is not uncommon for us to participate in thirty-mile hikes with full field packs. I don't know exactly what they weigh, but it feels like sixty pounds or more, and they get heavier as we go along! The closest we get to any real outdoor training is a bivouac (temporary camp), which is really not much more than learning to pitch a pup tent and dig a trench to use as a latrine.

60mm mortar

Other than live-fire training, we never do any training maneuvers, but

Pup tent

I do learn how to wash the dishes and scrub the pans. If I disobey an order, I will scrub the floor with a toothbrush or dig a foxhole, then immediately fill it. Yes, we do everything the army way.

We train on the rifle range, and I find that I am much more advanced than the average recruit. I have been hunting since I was 11 years old. I know I can shoot much better than I do at the rifle range, but the M1 I am issued is a worn-out weapon. The rifles used by recruits are semi-automatic weapons, but many are so worn out that we have to use them as if they are bolt action. Some of these weapons are so worn out they probably shouldn't be fired at all, but it is what we have to work with. Many of the guys in my platoon have never picked up or handled a firearm, much less a poor example of a rifle and are very inexperienced with handling them. I hear stories and see a few young recruits who have injured themselves because of lack of experience; black eyes and bruised shoulders are normal injuries for those who are not familiar with firearms. As mindful as our instructors are watching over us, one recruit gets a broken rib because

Shooter at the rifle range with an M1 Garand.

of his inexperience. We learn that cleaning our weapons is vital, and like everything in our lives, it has to be done the army way. A dirty rifle is of no use to any military man. We have to be able to disassemble, clean, and assemble it as if we are blind. If we damage or break our rifles, we will be charged eighty dollars, the cost of a new rifle. I currently only get paid fifty dollars a month.

Rifle cleaning at Camp Wheeler.

At the rifle range, we practice firing the rifle at distances of 100 yards to 500 yards. If you miss the target, a red flag called Maggie Drawers is raised, letting the shooter know he completely missed the target. There are a lot of bullseyes at the 100 yard line, but not many soldiers can hit

15

the target at 500 yards, and of course, we see the Maggie Drawers flying proudly at the 500 yard line.

As we advance through training, we begin our machine gun training on a Browning 1918. It is belt-fed, using a fabric belt that holds 250 rounds and is air-cooled and recoil operated. I quickly become an expert machine gunner. This is the weapon of choice for our live-fire training. Live-fire training is the most dangerous recruit experience. Imagine crawling on your back under barbed wire that is placed eighteen to twenty-four inches above the ground while live ammunition is being fired above you. You learn quickly to keep your head and your butt down as you travel a distance of at least 100 feet with bullets flying directly above you. I am thankful no one got hurt during this aspect of my training.

Discipline in the army is the top priority. Orders are to be followed, no questions asked. We all understand this. It is teamwork that gets things accomplished. In one exercise, we pick up a log in groups of 10 men and hold it over our heads. No one can slack off because we know that if we do, someone can get hurt. This is just one lesson of many in teamwork. The rest of my stay here is much the same: training, more training, and to relax, a little more training.

My seventeen weeks at Camp Wheeler is now coming to an end. The past four months have gone by with lightning speed, and at the end of our training, we are given a lecture by our commanding officer, a grey-haired 1st lieutenant who says we are infantry men, and no war has ever been won without our skills. Even with the past seventeen weeks of training, I have a feeling he knows what he is talking about, especially because of where the Army will be sending us. I believe he knows full well what we are up against and what the future holds. It's definitely not a bed of roses. We have been under his command day and night for seventeen weeks. With tears in his eyes, he bids us good luck and farewell. I know I will never see him again.

It is early February 1944, and I am going home for a few days to say goodbye to my family and friends. When I leave Camp Wheeler, I stop in

Macon, Georgia, for a short time. I'm not sure if it's because I have been surrounded by only men the past seventeen weeks, but Macon has the most beautiful women! I think all women are beautiful, some just more than others.

George on graduation day, Camp Wheeler, Ga.

As I board the train for home, I'm excited to get back to see my folks. I know I only have a few days before I will have to leave again on my journey, but I am thankful for the chance to visit. My trip back home is uneventful, but it does give me plenty of time to think. I'm excited to find where this adventure will lead me. I look up and see all the beautiful stars and the Milky Way floating above me. It reminds me of a hunting trip I took when I was young. So many stars lighting up the nighttime sky, you could never begin to try to count them all. I think about those cold, cold winter nights and the hardships that my family has endured, but mostly, I'm wondering where the winds of war will take me.

I arrive home, happy to be back with my family again. To me, so much has changed since I left for basic training, but in reality, I think I am the one who has changed. Now that I have returned, I can see the situation here much more clearly. To find work to keep thriving, my family is beginning to scatter. My older brother, Lester, has already left home two years ago to work for the Hercules Powder Plant in Radford, Virginia, and while I was in basic training my brother, Vernoy, who is two years

Back home with my family in Pound, Virginia, after basic training.

18

younger than me, also left home to work in Baltimore, Maryland, at a shipyard for the defense department. I spend time with my mother, father, and younger brothers and sisters. I think if this war lasts long enough, I'll eventually see all my brothers in the military.

I visit my grandma and grandpa. Grandpa has not changed at all. He is always happy to talk with me. He will keep me up all night if I don't insist on going to bed. Time is passing quickly, and it is almost time for Georgie to move on.

Four or five days go by, and my mind is battling with my emotions. I am torn between the adventure that lies ahead of me and the love of my family, especially my mother. I can't stop thinking about how she will worry about me after I am gone. I think of all my schoolmates who have already left for the service. Thankfully, my younger brothers are too young to go into the military, and although I may be too young as well, it is my choice to go. I feel like I am the warrior of the family.

The time has come for me to be on my way. I give each of my family members a hug. I hold my mom in my arms and give her a kiss goodbye. I pet my little dog, Trixie, on the head one last time, and off on this adventure I go.

The past week at home went by too fast. I am now traveling north to Fort Meade, Maryland, three hundred miles away. Fort Meade is the distribution center for thousands of soldiers awaiting orders and transport for active duty. I spend a few days here. There is not much for us to do. In the army, we spend a great deal of time waiting.

The time has come for me to continue this journey. I board a truck and am transferred to Camp Shanks, New York. Camp Shanks is called "Last Stop USA" because after this I go overseas. This camp houses 50,000 troops and spreads over 2,040 acres. It is the largest embarkation camp. Unbeknown to me, Camp Shanks will process 75% of those participating in the D-Day invasion. Leaving with the other men to catch the boat to Europe, I am one of 1.3 million soldiers who will process through this location.

Last Stop USA, Camp Shanks, New York.

Chapter 3
Rough Waters of the Atlantic

Troops walking up the gangplank on their way overseas. Courtesy of the U.S. Army Signal Corps. Courtesy of Golden Gate NRA Park Archives.

It is March 22, 1944. It is a cool evening, and here I am at the docks on the New York harbor. It's total darkness as I walk up the gangplank. It's not very steep, maybe 50 steps up to board the ship. There are ropes attached to either side of the gangplank that we use as handrails so we don't fall into the harbor. No one wants to start their journey in the water. I, like the other men boarding, have absolutely no idea where the military is taking me or what I will be doing when I get there, but hey, that's part of this young kid's adventure! This is a Liberty Class Cargo ship that has been converted for troops only. I can't really see this ship in the dark, but it is huge! It's 441 feet long, 57 feet wide and sits 19 feet deep in the water. We only have the starlight to see where we are walking as the port is in blackout mode.

A Liberty ship at sea. Photo credit: U.S. Office of War Information via Wikimedia.

On each soldier's back is a duffle bag with all his worldly possessions packed inside. Like me, the men boarding these ships are all fresh out of basic training with just enough training to know we are in the army. We are all replacements for the men who have been discharged for various reasons over the past months. None of us are currently carrying orders to attach us to any company or division. The only thing we have in common is that we are a group of men currently with no home. None of these men have a shoulder patch designating any outfit or group. I guess the sorting and assigning of men will happen as we get closer to our destination.

This ship is the beginning of a lifetime journey for this young 18-year-old kid from the Appalachian mountains. There are places and experiences awaiting me that I can't begin to imagine. Word is going around the ship that we will not see much of anything until we are seven hours out of port. The hours pass slowly. Seven hours later in the morning daylight, I get to see the Atlantic Ocean and the other ships in the water for the first time. In the early morning mist, I have no idea how many ships are in this convoy, but I am enjoying this great pond of water as I gaze out in the distance behind me one more time to the place I call home.

My ship is always in the front throughout the trip, first on the starboard side. To the rear, as far as I can see in this convoy, are ships. Two submarine chasers are out in front, patrolling to protect us and provide some safety from enemy submarines as we cross this huge body of water. Rumor has it we are traveling into the North Atlantic to avoid the Wolfpack. The Wolfpack is a term used for a mass attack tactic used against convoys by 8 to 20 German U-boats. As we get farther away from home, the ocean begins to get choppy, and then it really starts getting rough. I climb

German U-boat being towed into Gladstone Dock, Liverpool, after surrender to the Royal Navy. Courtesy of Wikimedia Coommons.

the steepest set of stairs I have ever climbed to go on deck, which is slow going. The turbulent waters make me work twice as hard going up the stairs. I reach the top and take a look out of the hatch. I step outside and take a short walk to the starboard side of this very large deck, hanging onto the side rails so I don't fall or get blown overboard by the wind and waves. I seem to do okay, but the ocean is relentless, and I decide it is best to go back down below.

As I enter the hatch to go back down, I am caught off guard by the light change. It has instantly changed from bright to very dim, and I'm not seeing very well. I have to stop for a moment to let my eyes adjust. As I'm standing here on the steps, a soldier comes towards me. He is really sick. He has vomit coming out of every orifice on his ghostly, white face. This is my kryptonite. Seeing a person as seasick as this poor soldier is all it takes to get me going too! I quickly move back through the hatch, make a run for the side of the ship, and let it go. In my sickened haste, I make the biggest mistake. I ran to the windward side of the ship. I never claimed to be a sailor! The peaches that I ate for breakfast come back up in my face. I'm not too happy about wearing my breakfast, but it sure feels better than trying to keep it in my belly. I go back down below, but I haven't finished getting rid of all my peaches yet. In fact, I think I'm just getting started. I run to the head (GI for lavatory), looking for an empty stall, but they're all occupied with guys sitting on the pot purging their bodies from both ends. I, too, am now seasick! I run around frantically searching. I need to find something or someplace to finish the deed. I run back to the head where there is a big, square wash basin for washing clothes. It is hidden from view with men shoulder-to-shoulder, their heads down, heaving up their breakfast. I must do something with everyone getting sick all around and nowhere to go. Like a long jumper preparing for his jump, I back up, take a good run toward the group around the basin and jump, landing on the top. There is a hole in the center of all the heads in the group, and I release the contents of my stomach down the center. No one mumbles a word; they just keep heaving.

I'm not feeling great after I empty my stomach, so I return to my bunk, which is a piece of canvas stretched between four steel poles. My bunk-mate and friend, Meade, is grinning. I say, "You, what are you so happy about?" Meade smiles and says, "I saw something really funny at chow." I'm wondering what could be so funny with everyone being seasick. The chow table is a long table, maybe 30-40 feet in length and about 2 feet wide with narrow boards running about 4 inches up on both sides to keep the mess kits from sliding off. We stand up to eat, hanging on to the

Stacked bunks aboard Army transport SS Penant.
Courtesy of the National Archives.

sideboards with one hand and eating with the other. Meade continues, "I was eating, and there was a sailor to my left. From the look on his face, I could tell he was not feeling well. The ship rolled to the port side, placing this ill-looking sailor over the guy's mess kit on the opposite side of the table. Just then this sick sailor loses control and vomits his predigested breakfast up in the mess kit of the guy across the table. I don't think he was very happy about the double rations he received." Yes, everyone is prone to getting seasick, Navy included!

During the next few days, the ocean is relentless. It goes from bad to worse. A voice comes over the intercom repeatedly, "No one on deck, no one on deck." Of course, my curiosity gets the best of me, and I decide I have a need to know why. I start making my way back to the deck to see what's going on up above. I begin climbing the stairs. I have to hold the handrail on the side of the hatch and hold on tight. I peek around the corner of the hatch at the deck to my right. A massive wave hits the port side of the ship. It's so big it engulfs the entire deck, going all the way across and over the starboard side.

To my left, out in front of the ships, are the two, small subchasers very busy at their job and wrestling with this rough ocean. At 110 feet long and 15 feet wide, these little subchasers and their crews have got to be some of the toughest! At times, the subchaser is completely engulfed in water except for a small part of the mast remaining visible. I imagine the beating the crews are taking in those small crafts! We are traveling at around 7 knots (8 mph), while the subchasers travel at about 18 knots (20 mph). The subchasers need to be quick because they run a zigzag pattern out in front of the convoy in an attempt to detect and warn the convoy of the Wolfpack's presence. I quickly go back down below deck. Hurrying down the steep, narrow stairs, I find Meade sitting comfortably. I climb into my bunk and try to get comfortable.

A few more days pass, and surprisingly, the sea begins to calm down as

Small wooden subchaser. Courtesy of http://www.navsource.org/archives/12/151009.htm

we get closer to land. A new message comes over the intercom, "Now hear this. Now hear this. Anyone who wants to volunteer to help take the ship back to the United States, report to the cabin." I look at Meade and say to my friend, "Meade, let's go for this." He looks at me, points to the small porthole and says, "See that land out there, that's where I am going. I've been on this ship for twelve days, and I am getting off this ship in Belfast, Ireland."

I begin thinking that we are going to make it after all. There have been many times on this journey that I have had my doubts, especially when the waves turned our ship on its side. The calm couldn't have come soon enough. A couple more days pass, and I'm feeling much better. I will be ready to eat at chow time, whenever that will be. I finally get a little food to stay down where it belongs, and I feel like climbing back up those steep stairs again to get another look. Stepping out on the deck is now a completely different experience. The angry ocean with its giant waves has become calm and peaceful as we move through the water toward the harbor of Belfast, Ireland. On the evening of April 4, 1944, as twilight begins to creep in, our ship docks and is secured. I, along with the rest of the passengers, get ready for "The Big Time," which is disembarking from this piece of floating steel. I take just a moment to give thanks to this special ship for safely bringing me three thousand miles through hellish storms and a rough ocean, especially the waters of the North Atlantic.

Chapter 4
Northern Ireland

When America entered the war, Northern Ireland became one large training camp for the Americans, as well as the Allied troops. For example, the 82nd Airborne Division was stationed in Ireland on December 9, 1943. There are also division-sized infantry bases, as well as hundreds of small military bases and outposts designed to train and house the troops in preparation for D-Day, the day the allied forces will invade northern France. Many of the Allied bases have no name, only numbers to designate them. These smaller bases are used primarily for training replacements, preparing them for the terrain and inclement weather they will be fighting in. Just before D-Day, 120,000 GIs are stationed in Northern Ireland at one time. During the course of the war, more than 300,000 American servicemen passed through on their way to combat.

It's early evening April 4, 1944, when I arrive at the docks located on Northern Ireland's shore in Belfast. I sling my duffle bag onto my shoulder and make my way to the gangplank. We begin to disembark in the darkness; it can't get any darker. We must each stay very close to the man in front of us. Everyone is quiet and serious; there's no monkey business, no funny jokes, just the sound of boots on the gangplank. Yes, as expected, a plane is flying overhead. I'm waiting to hear the explosion of a bomb. By the sound of the engine's drone, it's flying at a high altitude as it moves on past. We move slowly in the complete darkness until we reach the train. I am getting anxious. We can't board and get this train moving fast enough. "The Blitz" is very active and Belfast is one of its objectives. Boarding the train, I look toward the sky and see no stars. A long time has passed since I have seen any stars.

The darkness is so thick I can barely see the train car as I board. This old coal-burning train isn't much faster than the last one I rode on. I'm beginning to think this is one of the slowest methods of travel, but it is moving, bringing me through all these different cities to my destination, a small base in the northwest of Northern Ireland. We travel for a few hours in complete darkness until we reach a small town where I am transferred to a large, covered truck to continue my journey. I travel a short distance until I arrive at a small military installation. The base has no markers or any name posted, but the men stationed here call it Camp Somerset.

What a contrast of views as I climb out of the truck! There are old, rusty Quonset huts that are used to house the troops and a small, ancient, castle-like building that includes a ten-foot stone wall with broken glass imbedded in it to prevent it from being climbed. Someone must have built it for protection a very long time ago.

I get assigned to a Quonset hut and get a bunk. I take a few minutes to look around and check out my new temporary home. I decide to venture into a small village across the stream from the base. I go to the local pub and restaurant to get some chow. To be honest, I'm surprised by the language barrier I encounter. The beautiful young lady working there apparently is speaking English, but I can't understand a single word she says! I'm a Mullins: my ancestors came from Ireland, but with her thick accent, I can barely make out a word. It takes a minute, but we manage to communicate. Soon my ravenous appetite is quenched with the Irish version of pancakes, potato bread farl.

I talk with one of the locals, asking questions about my new surroundings. There's a beautiful stream nearby that I find interesting, and I ask if there are there any trout in that water. The response is, "Yes, mate, those are the King's trout!" The King's trout? Really? I have a little chuckle. This is the first time anyone has ever claimed fish ownership to me, and I find it humorous. I'm definitely not in the Appalachian Mountains anymore!

I enjoy my meal and the conversation, and then I return to camp to prepare for the day's activities. To start off, the troops are going to run a very challenging obstacle course, complete with ponds filled with water and ropes stretched across that we have to cross, hand over hand. We arrive at the course, and as we approach, I see a large net simulating the side of

GIs climbing a net to board a ship.

a ship, which we need to be able to climb up and descend. A long rope is tied high in a tree. We use it to swing across a small canyon, simulating a river. We tackle the course with vigor, and all is going well until my friend, Meade, traversing the hand-over-hand portion of the course, makes it about halfway over one of the ponds and starts laughing. He tries, but he can't hold on. He loses his grip falling into the water. He swims to the edge and comes out dripping with mud. I see he's an excellent swimmer, and where he's going, he'll probably need it. Meade just stands there with a silly grin on his face. This is our laugh for the day. Enough of the fun, now it's time for our hike.

This hike is going to be a long one. Along the way, I see the famous peat bogs of Ireland. There are two types of peat bogs in Ireland: blanket, which develop in the upland areas and raised, which is the type I see. Raised bogs are a little smaller in size and are found the midlands. Peat is used for fuel in the home. It is also used as insulation and mixed with textiles to produce blankets for livestock, as well as the peat moss itself being used as surgical dressings during World War I.

We pass the peat bogs and continue marching until we come in sight of a large bay where I see many ships anchored offshore. We keep on marching, and the hike continues. A short time later, I find myself back at camp. I'm exhausted and hungry. We eat chow, and then it's off to my bunk to get some rest.

Peat bogs in Ireland.

About two weeks have passed since I arrived here, and we are being assigned to our final units. Every soldier is being sent to a different location, each assigned specific job tasks within the different parts of the army services. The time has come for Meade, Shortt, and I to say good-bye, to part ways and continue our own separate journeys. We have only been at this base a short time. I am thankful for the time I got to spend with my two friends.

I'm hoping they both make it okay. The thought that I may never see or speak to them again is on my mind, but I suppress it. I hopefully will have the opportunity to communicate with them as we move forward in our travels. I haven't been told what unit I have been assigned to, but I'm guessing they will let me know when the time is right. For now, my orders are sending me by ship to Scotland and then by train to Reading, England. I board a truck which brings me back to Belfast, where I board a small ship that takes me to Scotland. I don't get to spend any time investigating this place, as I quickly board the train for my fifteen-hour ride to Reading, England.

Chapter 5
The Screaming Eagles

101st Airborne shoulder patch.

I arrive at Camp Ranikhet, Reading, England in mid-April. I see I have been stationed on a glider base. The barracks here are similar to the ones I was in at Camp Wheeler, Georgia, except they are single story and very empty.

I have been assigned to the 327th GIR (Glider Infantry Regiment), 101st Airborne Division, the Screaming Eagles. As I get settled in my new temporary home, I can't help but wonder about this place. There is nobody around. It looks like a deserted ghost camp. I keep myself busy exploring the camp. I make my way towards the chow hall, where I find a couple of cooks with two K.P.s (kitchen police) working in the kitchen. I talk to these men and find out the regiment is on a simulated invasion, but none of these guys know when they are due to return.

I am walking back toward the barracks when the sergeant of the guard approaches me. What a surprise! He assigns me to guard duty while I await the regiment's return. He takes me over to two damaged aircraft

 and says to me, "Private, your duty is to guard these gliders." He walks away, leaving me to guard the two beat-up CG-4A gliders. I walk around and take a quick peek at these derelict

Damaged CG-4A.

aircraft, and I say to myself, "Georgie, this is a fine mess you've gotten yourself into." I continue inspecting these piles of junk, and I can't imagine why anyone would care if these beat up planes get stolen. It's not my place to understand, and I tell myself, "This is not your way, this is the army way, so do your duty and protect these machines, even if they are never going to make it off the ground; it's your job." As I walk my post, guarding these beat up CG-4A gliders, I have plenty of time to inspect these motionless contraptions.

My inspection of the glider is almost complete. I try to imagine that it could be a nice airplane, but I can't even kid myself. This thing is a piece of junk! It has fabric for the skin covering and a steel tube frame and ribs. A typical glider, though not the ones I'm guarding, is forty-eight feet long and twelve and a half feet tall. The wingspan is eighty-three feet, it weighs 3,900 pounds, and has a maximum speed of 150 miles per hour. It can take off with a maximum weight of 7,500 pounds and can carry thirteen fully equipped soldiers, plus the pilot and co-pilot, or a jeep and five equipped soldiers, or one anti-tank gun and five soldiers, or a 75mm howitzer artillery piece, and anything else within its weight limit that can fit inside.

After completely inspecting this CG-4A, I try to figure out what each part of this aircraft does as it maneuvers through the air. I have always been fascinated by flight. I am looking forward to taking my first glider ride, but it better be a glider in better shape than the ones I'm guarding.

I am relieved of duty after about eight hours of walking around the two junk airplanes. As I am on my way back to the barracks, I notice many English girls standing on the outside of the base fence. Oh well, I guess these young women must be the girlfriends of the troops that are away on the simulated invasion. Walking through the compound to my barracks, I take note of the gardens that are between all the buildings and planted near them. No space is wasted. The gardens are very well taken care of, cultivated and manicured, and growing some of the most appetizing-looking vegetables.

A week of guard duty passes quickly. It's April 28, my nineteenth birthday, but it's just another day of guard duty. Cake? Wishes for a happy birthday? You must be kidding! The troopers of the 327th finally return from their simulated invasions. As they file into the barracks, I am happy to see these troopers that I have never met before. I do take note of the fact that instead of a lot of noise and fuss, the jovial sounds of being home, these troops entering the barracks are in a somber mood. No one says anything about where they have been or what they have been doing. This weighs heavily on my mind. Somewhere along the trail, as time moves on, I am speaking with one of the men who was on the training mission that I missed. When asked about the training, all he says to me is, "We got caught by the Wolfpack." At the age of 94, with the aid of modern technology, I finally find out where these men were and why nobody wanted to tell me about it. It is my understanding that these men were all out rehearsing a simulated invasion. The simulation was called "Operation Tiger" and was intended to prepare the men for the D-Day invasion of Normandy. This exercise took place near Devon, England, at Slapton Beach. The beach was chosen for its similarities to Utah Beach, and the exercise was to last from April 22 through April 30 and would involve over 30,000 troops. The first practice assault took place on April 27, and it ended poorly. According to my research, this exercise was plagued

Landing Ship, Tank LST 289 was loaded with men when a German torpedo hit it during "Operation Tiger". Photo: US National Archives.

by numerous problems; the first occurred the morning of the 27th when the troops training came under "Stupid Fire." What the military calls friendly fire is what I call Stupid Fire because there's nothing friendly about it; it's just stupid! Approximately 450 men lost their lives that morning. The order to use live munitions was given by General Dwight D. Eisenhower. I believe this was a bad decision: these men already had live fire training as part of military basic training, and I know that where we are going, we will be under heavy fire most of the time. Taking the risk of losing men in a simulation seems useless to me.

The next morning, the second practice landing was scheduled to take place. It was early in the morning when the convoy of eight LSTs (Landing Ship Tanks) were attacked by nine German U-boats. Two of the eight LSTs got hit with torpedoes and sank and a third one was badly damaged. At the end of the exercise, 749 men lost their lives in training. The LST convoy was supposed to have two ships assigned to provide protection, the HMS Azalea and the HMS Scimitar. The later, however, was in dock for repair. In the aftermath of this nightmare and because of the official embarrassment, as well as concerns over leaks just before the real invasion, the commanders decided to do a cover up; all survivors were sworn to secrecy by their commanding officers. Ten officers who had security clearances for D-Day were also missing, which concerned the top brass so much that they almost cancelled the real invasion. The U.S. military publicly acknowledged the losses months after D-Day, but the story was overshadowed by the news of the Allied invasion of Western Europe, and it remains little known, even today.

Now that the regiment has returned from their training, my real training begins. At 0600, the reveille bugle blows, and it's up and out of bed. From that minute until the taps bugle blows at night, we are moving at an incredibly fast, non-stop pace. Run, run, run! I have never run so much in my life. We do most of this running in the back streets of the town of Reading. A few weeks of training go by. It feels like we are training non-stop, every day and sometimes at night. The chow isn't the best, although I am always hungry when it's time to eat. It may not be the tastiest food, but there is always plenty.

I wake one frosty, brisk morning to our platoon sergeant entering the barracks and giving us the order to fall out in formation with all our gear in our field packs. He informs us that we are going for a glider ride. After weeks of being on this base and guarding a couple of these gliders, I've been anticipating this for some time now. I can't tell you how excited I am. We load up onto 6X6s and are trucked out to the middle of an open field. It looks like farm country to me, except for the CG-4A gliders that are sitting there. The crops have all been harvested, leaving only stubble and small dirt mounds from where they were planted. A C-47 is warming up a short distance away from the glider. I can see the tow rope that is attaching the glider to the plane. It's a big, fat, nylon rope, and it's really long, maybe 300 feet. We board the glider and get settled in our seats. We don't sit facing forward or aft. We sit facing each other on wooden benches along the sides of the glider's interior. It doesn't take too long for us to get off the ground. I can't describe to you the sensation of suddenly

Douglas C-47 takes off while towing a Waco CG-4A glider. Image courtesy of Wikimedia Commons.

Waco CG-4A glider. These were nicknamed "Flying Coffins". Courtesy of Wiki Commons.

being jerked off the ground. What's even stranger to me is that once we are off the ground, I take a look outside and notice that the C-47 has yet to leave the ground, even though we are at least 40 feet in the air. We are in the air for about 15 seconds flying before the planes wheels ever leave the ground. The plane finally leaves the ground, and we are being towed through the air. We fly behind the plane until we are about 1000 feet off the ground. At this point, the glider pilot releases the tow rope from the glider, and we are now flying on our own. As the C-47 leaves us, it gets quiet; I can only hear the sound of the wind as it rushes around the glider. The first thing I realize is that this glider can go nowhere except back down to the ground. I'm hoping this pilot is well-trained and will land this thing safely without killing us all. As the plane touches down on the ground, I am a little surprised by how smoothly and easily we landed. This isn't too bad at all! In fact, I actually enjoyed this ride immensely! I'm hoping we get to do this again soon! The only way I would have enjoyed this experience any more would be to have been the pilot flying this glider.

I'm very excited that I get a pass to go into town. Everyone going through the gate must have a pass. I find the town a very interesting place. I can see enough to recognize that the town has been here for a long time. From the old cobblestone roads to the very old houses that have real straw roofs, this place is rich with history. The local pub is a favorite place to visit, especially for the troops who are far away from home. I'm certain many a bartender will end up with grey hair from getting these GIs to leave the bar and go back to the base. The bartender is well aware that time is limited for American soldiers, and they need to be in camp at a certain time. The bartender is famous for saying in his British accent, "You bloody Yanks come over here. You drink our bloody beer, and then you complain, saying our bloody beer is no good, but you drink enough of the bloody stuff until you fall down and pass out on the bloody floor. Now come along, you bloody Yanks. You must go home; you can't stay here."

This pub looks pretty much like all the pubs I have seen so far. In my experience it's not a pub if you are able to see what you are drinking.

The Blitz is currently very active, so everything is completely blacked out. The windows are covered to the extent that no light from the building can be seen from the outside. There is just enough light inside to recognize the person you are talking to. The beer is a cool draft beer. A hand pump is at the bar, which pumps the beer from a barrel located in the basement. There is no refrigeration, although the beer is cold enough to satisfy the beer drinkers sitting here in the dark. I take a taste of this foreign spirit. It is nothing like moonshine, but it will do its intended job. I was never really a big fan of moonshine, but I am enjoying the taste of the local brew. I find the atmosphere here to be quite friendly. It's easy to start up a conversation with almost anyone. I am interested in talking to the Air Force personnel. I attempt to gather information from them about what they have seen where I am going. I get very little information out of them. One of the pilots, who has been flying over France today, says, "It doesn't look too bad at all." I should have had him expand on that statement. It's getting late, so back to camp I go to get some sleep.

As I walk back to the camp, I can feel these ancient old cobblestones under my feet. I imagine the early Roman soldiers in sandals marching on streets like these, although I know these roads aren't that old. These hard, uneven streets aren't the best for running, marching, or walking. There are a few fields around me. These open fields are planted with all kinds crops. We have been told by the military to respect the local farmers and not venture off the trail and trample their vegetables.

The next few weeks go by quickly. I can't believe I've been here over a month! It's been nonstop training, preparing me for the story written in the stars.

Chapter 6
Normandy

General Maxwell Taylor, commander of the 101st Airborne Division. Courtesy of the National Archives.

The month of June is almost here, and a large group of us are transported to a highly secret location. I feel like a prisoner because we are locked in a barbed wire stockade with unfamiliar soldiers guarding it. Their uniforms have no identifying patches or insignias to designate who they represent or their units. No one is allowed outside the compound. The first week of June, the commanding officer of the Screaming Eagles, General Maxwell Taylor, climbs up on a makeshift stage and gives us the latest news. In a powerful voice, he says, "Soldiers, this is it. On June 6, 1944, we are going to attack the beaches of Normandy. You are the best-trained troops in the world." He goes on and on, trying to motivate us for the occasion. He finishes up with, "Best of luck to you and to you replacements, do the best you can." The general's rousing speech leaves me feeling quite uncomfortable. I feel I am lacking in volumes of training, but I must agree with the general. He is all too aware that some of the replacements standing in front of him, including me, are unprepared for where they are going, but unfortunately, we will receive our real education as we proceed forward. I guess this is what is known as on-the-job training.

It's the first week of June, and we are trucked to the ocean. I climb aboard

LST Number 311. Landing Ship, Tanks were originally designed to transport tanks overseas. It's not quite as big as a Liberty ship, but at 382-feet long and 64-feet wide, it's not a small ship. We soon come in sight of an armada of ships of all sizes and shapes assembled off the south side of

The ship that brought me to Normandy, Landing Ship, Tank #311.

the English Channel, facing the beaches of Normandy, France. This is the largest group of ships ever assembled. The total number of vessels is 6,939, and they carry a total of 156,000 troops onboard. They range in size from small landing craft to the massive battleships.

There are many dirigible balloons above the ships. The dirigibles are attached to the ships with cables. Dirigibles are unmanned airships, similar to Zeppelins but with no engines onboard. Their purpose is to prevent enemy planes from getting in close enough to bomb or hit our ships with machine gun fire. Out on the horizon, I can see the smoke coming from the big battleships' guns as they bombard the beaches of Normandy.

The LST that I am on has many different pieces of equipment that we need to fight a war. There are ten Sherman tanks in the bottom, troops on deck, and troops down below. There are also jeeps, 6x6 trucks, weapon carriers, anti-tank guns, rations, water; everything imaginable to support

44

U.S. armada protected by dirigibles in Normandy, 1944. Courtesy of Wikipedia.

these troops. I have never seen so many different types of vehicles. As we approach Utah Beach, I see it is a busy place. Two mine sweepers appear behind my ship with a cable stretched between them. The cable is for detonating the big floating mines. When a mine is detonated, the explosion can shoot water into the air 40 to 50 feet high. Suddenly, everyone standing on the starboard side begins to yell. Not more than five feet away from our ship is one of those big floating mines with horns sticking out from all over it. It's a relief to see the ship begin moving away from that deadly, knobby bomb. If a ship detonates one of these mines, the explosion will blow a hole in the vessel that a jeep can drive through.

German floating contact mine.

We come to a stop about 100 yards

45

from shore. On the starboard side of the LST, I see a jetty with vegetation on parts of it that runs out into the channel about one hundred yards. Just past the beach is a German gun emplacement, which I take a close look at as soon as I go onto the beach. It is built into the cliff rock. It has no guns; the enemy must have moved the guns thinking that the allies would make their landing elsewhere. I am carrying my full field pack,

Troops making their way to the beach. Photo courtesy of the National Archives.

my folding .30 mm caliber carbine is hooked onto my belt, and I have two K-rations. There are different types of rations issued to military men. K-rations come in a box and are considered a survival ration. C-rations, or combat rations, as they are called, are a complete meal in cans. A-rations are fresh food rations.

We wear uniforms that have been impregnated with a chemical called CC-2 Chloramide. CC-2 was invented during the 1930s to help aid in combating gas attacks. The impregnated uniforms are heavy and make it almost impossible to run. I wish I didn't have all the extra weight attached to

.30 caliber carbine with folding stock.

my body. I am also helping pull a two-wheel cart loaded with ammunition. Two GIs are helping me, one using a rope on the opposite side of me, and one behind the cart, steering and helping me move it. Into the water we go! The water is really cold and up to my chin. I'm keeping an eye on the shorter soldiers to make sure they don't go under and drown.

The cart is much easier to pull as soon it is rolled into the water. We make it to the beach without any incident. The cart gets very difficult to pull through the sand as we begin climbing up the sand dune. The three of us struggle, pulling the cart as we climb up the dune to higher ground. A jeep comes along with three guys. I quickly attach my rope to the vehicle to help us get this thing up above the sandbar. All four wheels are spinning, and the driver starts complaining that the jeep is getting hot. It takes a few minutes with the driver griping and the tires shooting sand all over the place, but we finally make it to the top and out of the sand.

Three troops pulling an ammunition cart through town. Courtesy of the U.S Army Signal Corps.

It is dark, and I can hear an aircraft above us. I'm afraid it's a German aircraft, its pilot looking for a place to drop its bombs. By the sound of the engine, the aircraft is flying very low. I have no idea where I am, but I am told we are at the edge of a small village, Sainte Marie du Mont, Normandy, France, when we stop. There are so many vehicles that it creates a traffic jam. All these sitting vehicles are an easy target for an aircraft. It makes me nervous, and I wish we would move out.

All the vehicles are equipped with four very small lights, two in front and two in back, that are called blackout driving lights. The driver behind can see the two little lights in front of him. These lights are not visible from aircraft above. The German aircraft continues circling us, and every time the plane passes overhead, I think to myself, "This is the place the pilot is going to drop his bombs." We finally start to move out, but it's too late. It appears the pilot spotted our location. He continually passes overhead, and by the sound of the engine, I know that he is flying low. I suddenly hear a whistling, screeching sound. It sounds nothing like an airplane. It is the sound of a bomb being released. Faster than the bomb falls, we jump into a ditch at the side of the road. My anxiety ends as I breathe a sigh of relief after I hear the explosion a few yards away.

Front and rear blackout driving lights.

NORMANDY

We crawl out of the ditch and resume marching, crossing a small bridge. Dawn is just beginning to break, and it's light enough to see two bodies lying at each end of the bridge. Curiously, I move in closer and take a look. It is two German soldiers. I very cautiously walk up to the first one and give him a nudge with my boot to make sure he is dead. He's motionless. I walk to the other end of the bridge and nudge the other, no response. The reality of death sets in. I now realize this is not a game, this is for real! These are the first casualties of many I will see in the war. I'm sure glad they're Germans and not Americans. As I continue marching along, I can't stop thinking about those two enemy soldiers and how they met their destiny. I've experienced death before back home. I have seen both people who have died, as well as animals that I have hunted and killed, but nothing makes war more real than seeing these two dead bodies.

The morning has brightened up enough to see what's going on. There is a scattered forest on the right side of the road with parachutes tangled up in the trees like giant spider webs, blowing peacefully in the morning breeze. The parachutes I see are green camouflage, so this was most likely a supply or equipment drop, but the supplies and equipment are long gone. It was probably not so peaceful here a few hours ago with equipment falling all over the place and parachutes getting hung up in the trees.

We continue to travel until we reach a long, narrow field with the Douve River in front of us. It has many crooks and takes many turns as it travels on its way to the ocean. From this location, it flows to the north. Along the sides of the banks are large dikes to hold the water. There is a large field near the dike on the western side. A hay barn is in the middle of the field. We set up our defensive line along this dike. I am digging my foxhole a short distance from the barn when sniper fire begins.

I stand up just enough to see above the dike. I can't see any Germans. I know they are out there. A couple of foxholes away, Pfc. William H. Lemaster from Wayne County, West Virginia, peeks above the dike and says to his sergeant, "Where are they?" As the words are leaving his lips,

49

a German sniper fires a shot hitting Lemaster in the head, ending his life. This is the first casualty of C Company. At the same time, A Company is fighting a battle about 100 yards upriver to my right. I hear a mortar being fired from a field to our west, with one shell exploding in a field nearby. I move out in a hurry with a section of riflemen in the direction of the mortar fire. We capture two German soldiers firing the mortars. This is my first POW capture, and it goes without any problems. I turn the prisoners over to the proper authorities and return to the group.

On June 9, my squad, along with Lieutenant Stanley T. Skomski from Medina, New York, moves up along the northwest end of the field to dig our foxholes. No more than five steps away is a dead German soldier. I must check this guy. As I approach him, I can see he is a tall, blond-haired, blue-eyed German paratrooper. He is quite young, no older than me. He's a good-looking fellow, minus the bullet hole in the lower right side of his stomach. He's holding his first aid kit; it looks as if he was trying to patch his wound, which he failed to do before he died. Lieutenant Skomski says to me, "I think we will all sleep better tonight if we bury this guy." The lieutenant and I place him in a shallow grave and drive a stick for a grave marker at the head of the grave with his dog tags attached.

We rejoin our group, but before I dig my foxhole for the night, I must go look at something that I noticed earlier. I walk out into the field, and I see the remains of an airplane. As I get closer, I can see a body, or at least what's left of it in and around the wrecked aircraft, one of the crew, no doubt. I recognize the flight jacket, a sheepskin jacket that our airmen wear. As I return to my squad, I can't get the picture of what I have just seen out of my mind. I dig my foxhole and stay there overnight with very little sleep and not much to eat. It's slim pickings for breakfast because those two K-rations I was issued are long gone.

I am told we are going to cross the river after dark this evening. It seems to me that the sun sets very fast today. At twilight, my machine gun squad moves to the edge of the field. We watch as C Company files past us, pulling their rafts. The only noise that I can hear is the sound of our LCRLs (Landing Craft Rubber Large) sliding over the grass as we drag

Landing Craft Rubber Large, (LCRL) 10-man raft.

our ten-man LCRL. The raft has a top rope that is well-secured around the top edge of the boat. We use this rope to pull the raft as well as to hold onto in case someone falls into one of these deep holes. There is one other rope attached to the raft, the tie rope. It is mounted to the top center of the front of the raft and is used for securing the boat when we land. We drag the raft through the tall grass across the tide flats to the river. It isn't that easy, especially since the grass hides the large potholes scattered all over, but we cannot carry the boats with all these potholes. Sadly, I am the one who falls in a hole. It's dark and none of us can see where we are stepping. Suddenly, I'm four or five feet deep in a hole. I hang onto the rope, and I finally get a foothold on the sides of the hole and get out with the help of the other nine men pulling the raft.

It's just before midnight. The troops of C Company, minus their 60mm mortar men, are moving toward the river pulling their rafts in dead silence. No loud talking or any noise of any kind, no more than a whisper. My raft arrives at the edge of the river. I can see from the reflection that the other rafts are well ahead of us. I launch the boat which immediately starts turning around in circles. I quickly realize that the guys in this raft with me know nothing about rowing a boat because no one makes any attempt at getting our raft to travel in the direction we need to go. We are just spinning in a circle. I take command of the situation, doing my best to keep my voice down, and at the same time, I keep my focus on the fact that there could be a fast-firing enemy machine gun that could start firing any second. If it does, I will be going for a swim because we are easy targets sitting in this raft. I'm whispering orders to the men, instructing them on what to do to get this thing across the river. We are the last raft to be pulled up on dry land. I can't believe the Germans are not waiting for us.

I crawl to the top of the dike which is covered with stinging nettles. They are absolutely the worst. My hands instantly start itching and burning, a flashback to my boyhood days getting caught up in the uncomfortable stinging nettles around my home and in the fields. I crawl up to the left side of my platoon leader. I'm surprised in this blackness that I recognize him. My platoon leader, 1st Lieutenant Randol Patey from Dickson County, Tennessee, is now in a prone position to my right. Mortar rounds start coming in, and he says to me, "Our barrage is too close." With his flashlight, he signals toward the river to raise the fire. Lieutenant Patey then says to me, "Pass the word over the top." I pass the order over the top and it goes down the line, man-to-man, until the last man receives the order. It's over the top of dike and down the other side and into the field we go. Instantly, explosions fill the air, as a barrage from hell begins exploding all around. I am carrying my full field pack, my folding .30 caliber carbine, and a box of .30 caliber ammo. As we approach the field from the bottom of the dike, I begin firing my carbine with my right hand and carrying the box of ammo with my left. It's so dark I can only see the ground by the light created from our weapons fire and the barrage of exploding mortar shells hitting the ground and exploding all around us. There is so much noise and chaos. I am amazed to this day that any of us survived. Everywhere in front of me and to my left and right, there is no escape. I sense a round coming down to my left. It hits the ground to the left of a soldier directly to my left. He is dead, lying motionless next to me. I pause for a second while I process the shock of this man's death.

Through the flashing light from the exploding shells, I see the lieutenant running toward me. He grabs me by the coat, almost lifting me off the ground, saying, "Soldier, come on, you come with me." Oddly, the only thing I can hear, even above all the noise from the shooting of rifles and the explosions of the mortar shells, is the dying cattle. As the explosions stop, the lieutenant and I stand here for a second. It gets quiet. Even the cattle are quiet from their sounds of dying. Yes, it's as quiet as death itself. We can't see anything in this darkness, but just a few steps to our left in this narrow, green pasture of grass are at least forty of my brothers dead or wounded. There is no German 88 firing at us this night. I know these young men didn't get killed by booby traps or shoe mines. It is our own 60mm mortars. The morning report of June 10, 1944, is scrambled to the extent that it is unreadable. To this day and probably the rest of my life, this first episode of night combat will remain fresh in my mind. This is the atrocity of war at its worst.

The lieutenant and I crawl through a hole we find in the fence, stopping in a ditch on the other side of the narrow farm road. The lieutenant moves to my left disappearing out of sight. To this day, I find it surprising that I could recognize him in the dark. I don't ever remember seeing him again after this night's firefight.

I sit down. There is no noise, nothing but darkness. Many images begin flashing through my mind in just seconds. I have just experienced so many explosions that my brain, my body, and especially, my strength is overcome with the reality of the situation. I am having problems processing everything that has occurred in this first night of real combat. I'm mentally and physically exhausted. I know I need all my strength to carry on. I sit down to rest for a minute. The dawn of another day is just on the horizon, and I have yet to dig my foxhole. I am so tired, too tired to do anything except sit here and try to clear my head. My hands are so swollen from crawling through those stinging nettles last evening that they no longer feel like hands, let alone my hands.

The dawn of new day creeps upon me as we move to the outskirts of the tiny town called Brevands, France. We reach the top of the hill near a house with a couple of outbuildings. From here, I can see the Douve

River off to my left. I also see the armada of our ships out in the English Channel. Never before have I seen so many ships. The ships nearest to the beach do not appear to be very far away, maybe only a few miles. I see someone has nailed boards onto the trees that grow horizontally toward the Douve River. I can only imagine these boards were placed here by the enemy so they can climb the trees, giving them a way to observe the territory. I am certain this is where the sniper was when he killed Lemaster yesterday. I am very thirsty, but I am afraid to drink the water from the well nearby because it's possible the enemy could have poisoned it. A squad of our riflemen are moving toward the bunkers. Thirty-four years later in 1989, I am fortunate enough to visit one of these riflemen, 1st Sergeant James A. Gobles at his home in Kansas. He told me the Germans were excellent cooks. When his squad moved in toward the German bunker on that early morning, the Germans scattered and made a run for it. They were in such a hurry to get away from the American riflemen that they left their cooking pork chops behind. According to 1st Sergeant Gobles, the chops were warm when he and the other troopers helped themselves to some good-tasting pork chops.

I take a rest at the edge of the road. Sitting here, I see a large swastika that has been cut into the grass-covered slope. The sod that has been removed was most likely used to camouflage a nearby bunker. This swastika is enormous in size, at least ten feet across. I wonder what the true meaning and purpose of that unbalanced double "Z" thing is. I find out later that the swastika is a geometrical figure and an ancient religious icon from the cultures of Eurasia, where it was a symbol of divinity and spirituality. In the Western world, it was a symbol of auspiciousness and good luck until the 1930s when it became a feature of Nazi symbolism, an emblem of Aryan race identity, and as a result, is stigmatized by association with ideas of racism and anti-Semitism.

I'm thinking about this symbol when three troopers walk out of the brush. One of them has a .30 caliber machine gun on his shoulder. A sigh of relief passes that they aren't the enemy. In a flash, this feeling is gone. I don't recognize the three men. These guys are not part of the group of men that I was with yesterday or the day before. One of the three men

Swastika dug into the hillside. Drawing courtesy of Antonius Lapesara.

approaches me and asks me my name. I tell him "Mullins." He hands me a 31-pound machine gun and says, "Mullins, for now you are the machine gunner." He turns to the two troopers that are with him and says, "Private Avila, you are his ammo carrier and you, Private Soderquist, are to assist Mullins carrying the tripod for this machine gun." Private Ralph R. Avila is from Riverside, California, and Private Ray Soderquist is from Jackson, Mississippi. These two men and I make up about half a machine gun squad. There are two squads in a section. A machine gun section consists of two gunners, four ammo carriers, two tripod carriers/assistant gunners, two buck sergeants, a runner, and a staff sergeant to oversee them. I am missing three men to complete the squad. There is no sergeant or above to provide us leadership; all three of us are privates. We had two complete machine gun squads before we crossed the Douve River, so we are missing a total of nine men from the machine gun squads. In less than an hour, what is left of this company assembles, and we are on our way to Carentan.

We travel less than a mile when we leave the main road and are now on a trail going through the forest when I see giant craters in the earth, formed by the blockbuster bombs dropped by the Royal Air Force (RAF). These craters must be twenty feet in diameter and ten feet deep. We continue walking until we reach the edge of the forest. There is a causeway to our left that we follow on our approach to Carentan. When we get close

Crater created by a large aerial bomb.

to the town of Carentan, we enter a ditch with overhanging brush leading into town. As the men enter the ditch moving to the edge of town, the enemy opens fire, wounding the ones in front of the column. There is a steady call for medics. Our commanding officer, Major Hartford Salee, from Daviess County, Kentucky, begins ordering us to get out of the ditch and move forward. I don't think he ever stopped to think that moving out onto the exposed road leaves us completely exposed to the enemy. It is suicide. Even as inexperienced as I am and these other men of war are, we quickly realize that this is a bad decision. While standing on the road yelling orders at us to get out of the ditch, Major Salee takes a bullet to his leg. So much for up and out of the ditch. Later during this combat operation, we are warned to watch which way we are shooting. That being said, it makes me think that perhaps one of my compatriots had it in for the major.

One of our troops finds a route that leads through a cider cellar. As we enter the cellar, I notice the barrels are full and ready for service. I fill my canteen with apple cider. I am so thirsty I must have seconds. It does quench my thirst, but on an empty stomach the fermented cider doesn't sit very well. We move through the cellar and come out on the other side. It is higher ground near the back of a large cathedral with a steeple. The steeple currently is home to a sniper who is busy taking shots at our position. I set the machine gun on the tripod. As I finish, another soldier who is helping me grabs the trigger and sprays the steeple with half a belt of ammunition. This silences the sniper who is now dead or has made a run for it.

I begin to dig my slit trench. I haven't dug very deep. In fact, I am so tired I fall asleep. I wake up and notice that I am the only one awake among the few men that are here. I dig some more, all the while thinking about everything that happened last night and the other men who are supposed to be here with me. I can't get the missing men out of my mind. I hope they all made it to safety. I can imagine the giant ships with their large guns miles from here, out in the English Channel. They are being kept busy. They are so far away I can't hear them firing, but I can hear the swish-swish noise as the massive rounds pass just a few feet above me as they travel into the town of Carentan. I keep digging in. It feels like I have been digging for hours, and the hole is no more than twelve inches deep. I am on my knees while I'm busy digging. I pause to say a short prayer. I really don't know what to pray for; I'm only asking for something I can hold on to, something to give me strength and faith in myself and this mission. I stand up and turn. Behind me, just a short distance away, stands Jesus. Streaks of very bright light appear from all over his body, except his right hand and part of his arm. He takes a few steps towards me, offering me his hand, but he never touches me. This vision disappears in a blink of an eye.

The big rounds keep hissing through the air above. A thought about my grandpa flashes through my mind. My grandpa was also named George. When I was growing up, he told me a little story on many occasions. He would tell me that just a few days after I was born, he walked more than twelve miles into Kentucky to see his grandson, George. When he arrived, he found a baby in quarantine, baby George. I was in a room by myself. The windows and doors were sealed. Only my mother and the doctor were allowed to enter. My grandad could only see me through a window. When he returned to his home in Virginia, he said to my grandma, "We will never see little George alive again." I don't know why I was in quarantine. I guess at the time it didn't really matter; my family was just happy I was alive. I guess I should have asked my mom back when I had the chance, but for now, I am thinking, "Grandpa, I am very much alive, although I could be living on borrowed time." I remember stories about the American Indians and their sacred ground. I feel my native heritage calling to me, and like my ancestors did many years ago, I claim this small spot of earth as my sacred ground: this tiny little space of earth near this large cathedral in the town of Carentan, France.

With my prayer answered, I feel renewed. I know in my heart and soul that my life has already been recorded, perhaps somewhere among the millions of shining stars. Whether good or bad, it's my story, placed in the heavens. The stars, like our lives, shine as brightly as ever, although, thanks to this war, I can't remember the last time I saw the stars in the night sky. It's like they are hiding, refusing to watch the burning, smoking fires and self-destruction of mankind's wars.

I finally fall asleep but am awakened in the early daylight by the noise of machine gun fire. The German soldier, as he quickly fires his machine gun, definitely didn't sleep in today. Just a few steps away there is a mound of dirt with a hedge on top of it; a path has been cut through it. The enemy's bullets are coming through the opening. The troopers wait until a bullet passes, then make a dash through the opening. I'm off to the side of the opening. I lift my machine gun over my head and throw it over the hedgerow and over I go, tumbling with my machine gun across the ground on the other side. I begin crawling up the ditch that is on the opposite side of the hedgerow leading me to Carentan. I'm pulling the machine gun along with me while crawling through human waste, left because someone didn't use his shovel.

It's early morning as we enter Carentan. I have never seen so much destruction in one place. As I walk along the streets of Carentan, I can see rubble standing in large piles where there once were buildings. Smoke lingers from the explosions. Just recently there have been many battles raging between our troops and the German soldiers, but so far this morning, it appears as if the enemy decided to retreat and get the hell out of this town of Carentan. I am surprised that we meet very little resis-

Paratroopers cautiously move through Carentan. Photo courtesy US Army Signal Corps.

tance. The few people on the street are looking for loved ones as they speak with the other survivors about the mayhem that has just passed.

We pass through Carentan at a fast pace, leaving town and advancing through the countryside. I see one of our paratroopers lying dead on the side of the road. I take a few seconds looking at this trooper, completely puzzled. I don't know how he can look so clean. It's not the norm for the paratroopers I've seen out here. He looks as if he just came out of the shower. He's clean-shaven, his uniform appears spotless. Everything about him looks perfectly in place, except that he has no life in him.

I hurry to catch up with the column. We are within half a mile of the Village des Ponts Douve, France, when we run into enemy resistance, and our bazooka man gets killed. This doesn't make any sense. Normally, a bazooka man wouldn't be up front with the scout. Bad tactics, if you ask me. As we move through this small village, suddenly, it comes alive with a loud explosion and rifle fire. A German comes forward carrying a white flag. He throws a "potato masher", a German grenade, wounding two of our soldiers.

Two German infantrymen with a potato masher. United States National Archives Identification Code: 242-GAP-286B-4

We get the news that we are fighting the Russian Liberation Army, a group composed of Russians who are collaborating with Nazi Germany. These soldiers were mostly former Soviet prisoners of war but also included veterans of the anti-communist White Army. Seventy-three years later while giving an interview, I finally learn the truth. This soldier who didn't honor the white flag was neither German nor a Russian from the liberation army; he was a Georgian from the Soviet Union. Many Georgians were so against Stalin that they joined the German army in hopes of restoring Georgia's independence. This particular fellow was just one of many who chose the wrong side of history. He gets what he has coming to him. Our riflemen take him down with a rain of bullets.

At the edge of the village, we meet up with the 29th Infantry that is moving through. Without much care, I drop this heavy machine gun to the ground. A lieutenant with the infantry approaches and says, "What I would give for an outfit like you guys." I just don't see what this lieutenant sees in me and the other ones in this Airborne infantry that he doesn't have in his own soldiers. I admit that we do look rugged. My only uniform is heavily soiled. So much filth is impregnated in it, it probably weighs an extra five pounds

As darkness closes in, we move out, carrying our wounded. This is very difficult for me to do. I am carrying more than I weigh. I'm exhausted, and what little strength I have left is barely enough to keep me going, but I know these soldiers need to be brought to safety. As we move past the opposite side of the village, there are many trenches and emplacements. It is unbelievable to me that the German's decided to leave instead of trying to hold this town.

We come to a halt, and I waste no time setting up my machine gun at the edge of the road. I'm exhausted. I try to sleep, but sleep has long been forgotten. I restlessly doze in and out of consciousness. At daybreak, I open my eyes as I hear someone talking. Even in my half-asleep state, the words come through loud and clear. A soldier says, "I can see the Germans entering a house that is about one hundred and fifty feet away."

The morning is fully upon us, and I am coming alive. I pause for a second, rubbing my eyes and am relieved to see a few armored vehicles in the adjoining field, including three tank destroyers with the big, white stars on them. Our troops!

We find a vehicle for our wounded, then return through the same fields we passed through yesterday. We continue to travel south of Carentan. We begin setting up another position that isn't in the best location, but it will have to do. A tank from across the field is firing almost point blank on our position with the shells tearing the ditch across the road to pieces. We get the order to move out because very soon our men are going to tear this place apart with a "rolling barrage." Barrage fire is not aimed at specific targets; it is aimed at areas in which there are known or expected targets. A rolling or creeping barrage is when batteries of artillery concentrate artillery bombardment over a wide area. The artillery usually fires at a steady rate, using high explosive or historically, shrapnel shells. A barrage might be from a few or many batteries or rarely, from a single gun. We continue traveling south, moving at double time to another defensive position. 1st Sergeant Kenneth J. Whalen from River Falls, Wisconsin, approaches me and gives me the usual orders. "Mullins, take your squad, go out in front and set up a machine gun outpost. Make sure you have good grazing fire." My squad of two men and I waste no time. We place the gun on top of a dirt hedgerow about four feet in height, overlooking a green field about four hundred yards from the German line. I dig my foxhole. This is a good one. It's deep, with plenty of room. Soderquist is to stand guard during the first part of the night. I cannot sleep. I keep waking up so I go check on Soderquist. I find him asleep with a blanket over his head. I shake him awake and not using the most pleasant words, give him a piece of my mind. I know it wasn't the friendliest way, but he is responsible for our lives!

At the break of dawn, I must investigate a farmhouse which is nearby. I knock on the door. An old lady, probably someone's grandma, answers the door. She is all by herself. This is a battle area. She has no business out here alone. I say something to her in French. I know enough French to get me in trouble, and this is the case at present. She goes crazy. She seems so mad at me, as if I had just kicked her dog. She just won't stop screaming at me. Fine, Grandma, have it your way. I walk away as she continues her harangue in French. I get a few yards away from her and her yelling when a large black and white dog approaches and decides to make friends with me.

We move quickly, the large dog leading the way back toward my foxhole, when suddenly rounds start falling on the machine gun squad from our own guns. Stupid Fire from our own artillery. The dog and I start running toward the foxhole; the dog wins the race as he dives to the bottom of the hole, scared stiff. I can't explain the fear I feel as I hit the hole as quickly as a streak of lightening. I am at the bottom of the hole, lifting this large dog and throwing him out of the foxhole. Immediately, he is back in the hole, lying on top of me, giving me protection from the shrapnel raining down around us. I flash back to being a young boy hunting rabbits. I remember how fast those poor little buggers would run, hoping to beat me to their rabbit hole and live to see another day. Now I have become that rabbit, running and hiding in my hole, hoping to save my life to see another day. I look behind me. I see no artillery men in the area; there is not one observer or spotter in the area to give any feedback to the artillery. It's like no one cares. I am upset and angry, friendly fire my butt! Stupid Fire is all too well known and should never happen! It's a good thing there is no observer here at this moment. I could quite easily mistake him for the enemy. It's unacceptable to me that an outfit could be so stupid as to rain bombs down on their own. After a few minutes of venting my anger, it looks as if the artillery observer finally gets it right. I see German medics running to help their wounded after our artillery tears their hedgerow to pieces.

The enemy doesn't attack, and we hold our position until we get the order to move out. I pat my new friend, the dog, on the head, bid him farewell, and we are off on our way south to set up another defensive position.

We stop at the edge of a country road. Avila and I begin digging our foxholes. Chaplain Newton G. Crosby from Alexandria, Virginia, approaches. He has a very pleasant manner. I notice his smile, as there aren't many smiles

Chaplin Newton G. Crosby

63

from the men around me these days. He asks me "When have you last written home?" I tell him, "Chaplain, it's been far too long for me. Maybe

My brother, Harold Mullins.

before we left England." He looks at Avila and Soderquist. "How about you two?" Their response is the same as mine. He takes our addresses and promises he will get letters sent off to our parents. He shakes hands with each of us, bids us farewell, and he is on his way. We return to the digging. I can't stop thinking about my lack of writing back home to my mom and family. When I returned home after the war, I find out that my brother, Harold, would walk two miles every day to the post box just to see if his brother, Georgie, had written home. I'm glad I don't know that now. It would make me feel worse than I already do about my lack of communication. Harold is such a smart one! To this day, he knows my military number. He had memorized these eight numbers as a young boy so he would know if it was a letter from his big brother. I feel bad that I've left them all to wonder. I'm most certainly in the doghouse this time. I don't know where the time has gone since leaving England. I haven't seen any writing paper since I left there, and I don't know what I would do with a letter if I did write one. There is no pony express on this trail, let alone any mailman. It's been over a month since I wrote to my mom. She will be worried sick. Hopefully, the chaplain will write to her. He does make good on his promise, but by the time the letter arrives home, it's been months since my mom has heard from me.

20 June 1944
Somewhere in France

Dear Mrs. Mullins,

                    Just a brief word to let you know that I saw George today. As you know his life these past few days has been strenuous but in spite of it all he is feeling fine. This outdoor life seems to agree with him. He is proving himself the fine soldier that we knew he would be and you have every reason to be proud of him.

                    The Lord has been with us and watching over us and we ask a continued interest in your prayers. Although George is not able to write much these days, your letters mean a great deal to him. I shall continue to be interested in George.

          May the Lord bless and confort you, I am,

                    Most sincerely,

                    Newton G. Cosby
                    Chaplain USA

Chaplain Crosby's letter to my mom.

I'm standing in my foxhole. I look down, and I can't believe what I see crawling up my leg. It's a damn death bug (European carrion beetle). These are by far one of the nastiest-looking bugs I have ever seen in my life! I quickly knock it off and start yelling at it, letting it know I'm very

Carrion Beetle (Death Bug)

much alive! I've been shot at, bombed, crawled through all sorts of muck, and now I have bugs that feed off dead animals crawling up my leg and around in my foxhole! This is one of many reasons that military men blouse their trousers! I know it's time to move out again because I'm starting to yell at the bugs.

We are moving south as we travel on a road through green pastures. I can't help thinking about growing up in farm country where the fields feed our cows and other livestock. My mind and stomach can't stop thinking about eggs, butter, and milk; all those wonderful food items that come naturally to a farm boy. We stop for a break, and like a gift from the heavens, I see a cow near a barbed wire fence. I haven't had any fresh milk since I left the States. I decide to climb over the fence and walk over to this old girl, eyeballing her as I approach. I gently speak to the cow, giving her a little pat on the back. I see she is gentle and very calm with me. I unbutton the pouch of my canteen cup, squat down next to "Old Buttercup" and give a squeeze. Almost immediately, my cup is running over with nice, warm, foamy milk. I take a good, long drink. Never in my life has milk tasted so good! I look behind me and see at least ten guys lining up with their canteen cups in hand, asking me if they too can have some of this cow's milk. Well, I sort of like this group of guys and know how much they will appreciate a fresh cup of milk. I take each man's cup and fill it until Old Buttercup is dry. With our bodies now satisfied with milk, I climb back over the barbed wire fence and head back to the road to regroup with the column.

We arrive at a bivouac area where we stop and set up camp to stay for a few days. After a couple days here, I begin to feel almost like myself. Today is a special day because instead of a 6x6 taking me where people are trying to kill me, I get to ride on one of the trucks to the ocean for a swim.

We arrive at the ocean where the weather is warm, but the water is cold.

No complaints here, at least it is water. I grab a bar of soap and enter the water. It's been so long, I'm not sure I know what a bath even feels like. I quickly find out that soap won't to stick to anything in this salty brine of an ocean, but I do the best I can to get clean. I think the last time I really got clean was two weeks before leaving England. That was over a month ago.

The ocean is a new experience. I never swam in the ocean before. I enjoy the swim very much, although at my naive young age, I know nothing of the sea monsters that swim quietly near the surface, those cold-blooded, man-eating monsters known as sharks. Today, however, none of us are on their breakfast menu. The men and I spend a short time in the water and look much more human. We load back up on the trucks and proceed back to camp. We spend another week or so at this camp. The camp has a field kitchen, and I'm thankful for hot meals. Anything is better than a K-ration!

We hear that our troops have taken the Normandy Peninsula and have the vital seaport of Cherbourg. I prepare to leave Normandy with a good attitude, pleased with what has been accomplished.

I had written a letter to my friend, Edward Shortt, a little while back. Today it is returned to me with the word "DECEASED" written on it. He is one of thousands of soldiers that do not make it out of Normandy. I pause for a moment to think. What a terrible price we pay for every inch of soil we liberate from the German regime. Seventy years later, while doing research for my book, I find out this was bad information, Private Edward Shortt actually died in Germany on November 19, 1944.

Back at the bivouac area, we hear the rumor that we are going to go to our base camp, Camp Ranikhet, Reading, England. We load up onto the 6x6 trucks and ride to the Utah beach area, near the place we landed a month ago. To my surprise, it looks nothing like it did when I arrived. The Allied forces have just withstood a fierce, violent sea storm. In fact, it was one of the most powerful, destructive sea storms to hit the beaches of Normandy in the last eighty years. Ships of many sizes lie on their sides.

Ramps, docks, and assorted materials and supplies for war are in great piles.

It is as if the Gods of War are angry at us for challenging what is supposed to be the most powerful fighting force in the world.

I am certain the Germans were taken by surprise with the ferocity of our fighting. Historically, the German army would destroy any force or obstacle in its path. They seemed to be well-prepared for action on the beaches, fabricating cross sections of steel structures and floating the large, spooky mines for miles.

I know the Germans are also surprised that the Atlantic wall has been blown to bits by the Allied forces. This wall took the enemy two years of sweat and blood to build. The Allied forces have destroyed it in a matter of days. Millions of dollars worth of German big guns are in pieces here, blown up by the US engineers to prevent the Germans from ever using them again. The last time I was here, I had to walk through the water with all my gear, but recently the Allies have constructed some makeshift docks which make it much easier to board the ship to head to base camp. We land in Wales and board a train to Reading.

We arrive at Camp Ranikhet near Reading, England and are welcomed by our wounded compatriots, as well as the locals. It feels like heaven on earth here! A hot shower, a real bed to lie my worn, tired body down. A chow hall with real, cooked food! A hot meal is just what the doctor ordered. Nothing against rations, I'm forever thankful I had them, but I must be honest and say that as long as I live, I will never miss those half-cooked, low-grade potatoes!

I am very happy to be back in England. Our days are filled with lots of exercise to help build our stamina. It's run, run, run, all the time. Many of the soldiers get passes to go anywhere of their choice, anywhere, of course, except home.

Chapter 7
A Short Romance

Statue of Eros, the God of Love, in Piccadilly Circus.

The Three Musketeers, Mullins, Deryneoski, and Avila, in London, 1944.

When I finally get a shower, a shave, and clean clothes, I almost feel like a new soldier. Avila, his good friend from back home, Frank Deryneoski, and I get a week-long pass. We decide to go to London. We hear this city is large, currently the largest city in the world. It is over forty miles wide. It's been years since I heard about Germany first bombing London. It is referred to as the Blitz, short for the German word, blitzkrieg (blitz meaning lightning and krieg meaning war). They are short, fast, intensive, and sudden military bombings. London has survived these bombings for several years now. I can see the results all around me. Once beautiful brick buildings where people lived and children played now lie in ruin. The business and living heartbeat of everyday life is now a memory. What remains are large piles of rubble and bricks, permanently etched with the color of intense heat and smoke as a reminder of the tragedy. Much of the city of London lies silent in the rubble, block after block, where 43,000 people eventually perish.

A number of years has passed since the English pinned the name Yank on the American soldier. During World War II, the Yanks become something of a celebrity. The fear of falling under the rule of Germany's Nazi regime has never left the minds of the English people. There is, however, an atmosphere of good times in the air, although hard times exist all around us. There are food shortages of all kinds, soap is in high demand, and toothpaste is considered a luxury.

The streets are also scattered with men from the American military. Never have I seen the actions of soldiers so spontaneous, crazy, and wild as I am seeing right now! The American soldiers need no encouragement, but of course, there is quite a bit coming from the local women who are very happy to see these men. As far as I can tell, everyone is having a good time. Thousands of American soldiers marry English women. There is a saying that is heard quite often and directed at the American soldier here in London: overpaid, oversexed, and over here.

The soldiers running around bring a sense of a carefree world, but most of them are really living life as if it's their last day on earth. The reality of war makes a person realize your time could come at any second, it could be tomorrow, or the next day. The question of one's existence is constantly running in the background of most of our minds. No one knows if the next mission will be the last for the B-17 soldier flying over Germany. I think about all the paratroopers. There is no guarantee any of them will survive their next jump. There are so many infantry soldiers in their foxholes. Each one of them knows the risks of being bombed, shot, or buried in the hole they dug. I think about the sailors, such easy targets stuck on their ships with the constant fear with of being chased by the Wolf Pack on the high seas. I think about me and my team. If the glider we travel on goes down, as many do, I know not many will survive. The best advice is the advice I see all around me: forget about these fears, have a good time, and live these days as if they are your last.

After a couple of days wandering around London, these Three Musketeers decide it's time to go to a different city which turns out to be Nottingham, England. This is one of the cities the children of London were taken to during the height of the Blitz. Although it is a very interesting place, we decide not to stay here very long. It's far too crowded for our liking. We decide to go back to London and make our way to the train station. As we board the train, I see an American soldier I recognize. Standing close to him is a beautiful, blonde-haired, fair-skinned young woman. She reminds me of a movie star, minus the make-up. Truly a natural beauty! This petite blonde sits down on the train near me as I get settled for the journey. She introduces herself as Kay Martin. She wastes no time in telling me she doesn't care for the soldier she is with and doesn't want to be near him. I say, "Stay with me, you have nothing to worry about." I introduce myself as George. She asks if I have a middle name. "Yes", I say, "It's Kenis." She replies, "We have had too many King Georges here in England. If you don't mind, I will call you Kenis." We enjoy our train ride back to London as we speak, sharing and exploring each other's worlds.

She invites me home to meet her family. I quickly accept and wish the other Two Musketeers a good night. We arrive at Kay's home. Her family has many questions to ask this young soldier. They want to ensure that my intentions are honest. We talk about our families and our homes. Kay has so many questions, enough for me to know she is very interested in me. It is becoming a very pleasant evening.

The next day, I pick up Kay, and we go on an adventure to take in the sights and experience London. I am happy to be with Kay. She is a wonderful guide. We go to Buckingham Palace, and I witness, first-hand, the changing of the guard. We travel a short distance away to Piccadilly Circus. What an amazing and interesting place it is. There are so many different shops. There are people giving speeches, talking above all the

The changing of the guard, Buckingham Palace, London.

noise, as they try to get money to rebuild this or that. Kay and I sit down on the beautiful lawn in the park, not paying very much attention to what is going on here at Piccadilly Circus. We are much more interested in each other. I try to relax and let what comes naturally happen, but like most young soldiers, I get too close, too quickly for her comfort. She is quick to remind me of my place. She tells me in her very kind, loving way that she is saving herself for the one she will someday marry. I am not too happy with her statement, but because I respect and care so much for her, I don't press the issue.

We spend the rest of the day just talking and enjoying each other's company. My time here is quickly coming to an end. Soon it will be time for me to return to camp, thirty miles south. As the sun fades slowly in the west, we return to her home. I go inside with her and chat with her family until it's time for me to get back to the base. I bid Kay and her family a goodnight. Kay walks me out. I give an affectionate kiss to my Kay, get her address, promise to write to her, and tell her I hope to see her again soon.

With a heavy heart, I walk back to the train station. It's not very long before I am boarding the train to go back to Camp Ranikhet in Reading.

A SHORT ROMANCE

What a situation I am in! I really like this girl, but my life is very complicated as a young soldier. I know I am going to battle again, and I know that there is no place for a heartbroken soldier on the battlefield, nor do I wish to have a wife or a girlfriend who will be heartbroken or worried about me.

I arrive back at the base, and as I enter the barracks, I see we have a full house of soldiers trying to finish their chores before the bugler sounds off with Taps, his last order of the day. I get to my bunk and find I have a surprise that's been waiting for me. The tall, southern Texan I had seen boarding the train with Kay back in Nottingham approaches me and says, "Let's go outside. I'm going to beat the hell out of you." I say, "What's your problem?" He replies, "You took my girlfriend." I say, "Your girlfriend?" This sort of macho gibberish goes on for about five minutes. I don't know what this big guy saw in me, but he backs down and goes back to his own bunk. The tall Texan never gets a chance to beat the hell out of me nor does he ever get another chance with my Kay.

A couple weeks go by and I get another pass. I am so excited to see Kay. I get to London, only to find my sweet Kay is not feeling well. She probably caught a cold sitting in the damp grass at Piccadilly. With a heavy heart, I think about returning to base, but instead I decide to go visit my cousin, Woodrow, who is in the Air Force and currently stationed in Nottingham. It will be nice to see a family member so many miles away from home. He takes me to visit his girlfriend, who later becomes his wife. After our visit, we return to the barracks for a while. I enjoy my visit, but again, it's time to get back to the base. Before I leave for my long trip back to Reading, I stop to use the latrine. A pilot approaches me and says, "Hey, trooper, where are you going?" I tell him, "I am on my way back to Reading." He smiles and says, "I'm on my way to London. Come with me." Talk about luck! The next thing I know, I'm getting on board the most beautiful aircraft in existence: a B-17 Flying Fortress! The first thing I notice as I get on board is that I have to step across the open bomb compartment bay doors. We take off, and I find it quite interesting to be looking down through the bay doors that are open, seeing all the trees, towns, and cities from the air! Things sure do look small

B-17 Flying Fortress Bomber. Still one of the most beautiful planes ever created.

from my perspective. It's a great thrill to feel the rumble of engines as I fly through the air! I have been on a couple of gliders, but this is my first experience in an aircraft with engines.

Another week goes by, and I get another pass. Right back to London I go, certain I will see my Kay. I invite her out to dinner. Kay and I go to a very nice restaurant for dinner. Even while I am enjoying myself, it seems as if I can't get away from this war. As we sit in the dining room, we hear a humming sound that is coming from an engine overhead. Kay says, "Kenis, it's a buzz bomb." I really don't get too excited because one of the things I have become most accustomed to over the past month is having artillery and mortars dropping their explosives all around me. All the noise in the restaurant stops as the buzz bomb passes overhead. It's quiet, so quiet I can hear a pin drop. The humming stops, and a few seconds afterward, we hear the loud explosion of the five-hundred-pound bomb that has just touched down, blowing yet another part of the city to pieces. We finish our meal and I take Kay back home and return to my hotel.

The following morning, I board a train to take me back to Camp Ran-ikhet.

Flying buzz bomb is pulled by soldiers on sledges to its launching position. Bundesarchiv, Bild 146-1975-117-26 / Lysiak / CC-BY-SA 3.0

Chapter 8
The Longest Ride

I am so thankful for the month-long rest I just had, but now it's back to business. Since I returned to Camp Ranikhet, my days are filled with serious military training that sometimes extends into the night. We are constantly being placed on alert and preparing to make airborne landings ahead of General Patton's Third Army. This happens several times but never materializes because his tanks and infantry are moving so fast that we can never get organized quickly enough for the operation.

I am beginning to see just how many different personalities there are here in the military. We all dress the same, but no two men act alike. In fact, they run from wild and crazy to calm and easy going. There are many new faces to be seen in the barracks as new replacements are attached to my unit. One of the replacements who inspires me is Private First Class Otis B. Cady from Mason, Michigan. He is Chaplin Crosby's new side-kick and one of the friendliest people I have ever met. Cady always looks like a first-rate soldier and has a kind word for everyone. To me, he's one of those people that a person could easily become attached to. He is known as "The Sky Pilot," but to us, he is much more than a soldier; he is our right-hand man with a direct connection to God or as close as we are going to get to one. I also have replacements added to my machine gun squad, Sergeant Carl Ewell and Private Herschel C. Parker, both from Dallas, Texas. Parker has acquired much experience and training already, more training than I ever got. He was a National Guardsman for a number of

Private First Class Otis B. Cady

Pvt. Herschel Parker   Sgt. Carl Ewell

years. He tells me that he was recently a staff sergeant, but he got in some trouble and is now a private just like me. Soderquist has been replaced on my squad by Private Joseph Henn from Petersburg, Nebraska. I feel certain that Henn will do a good job. Finally, there is an older guy by the name of Private Hoffman. I don't remember much about him because we never got that close. With Avila and me, we have a complete machine gun squad for the first time since before the Douve River crossing in Normandy, France.

On September 11, 1944, I, along with thousands of Airborne soldiers, receive the news of an Airborne operation that will become one of the largest, most expensive, deadliest, and longest lasting battles that the Allies have ever known. This operation is called Market Garden. The Allies hope this will speed up the end of the war by at least six months. Market Garden is primarily planned and led by the British. It includes the 101st and 82nd Airborne Divisions, the British First Airborne, and the Polish First Independent Parachute Brigade, who are temporarily attached to

This is my armband. All 82nd and 101st Airborne troops that participated in Market Garden wore one.

the British Airborne. According to *Wikipedia*, the United States and its allies had 41,628 men involved in this operation. There are no final numbers of how many Germans are involved, but what numbers are available show an equally large group. History tells us that Operation Market Garden started on September 17, 1944, and finished on September 25, 1944, but the truth is this operation lasted for seventy-two days. I know because I was there. The intent of Market Garden was to capture key bridges so the Allies could control the Rhine. There were many unfavorable circumstances that began stacking up from the start of Operation Market Garden. Despite their heroic efforts, the Allied forces ultimately failed to achieve their objectives and sustained devastating losses in the process. However, ask the liberated people of Holland. They will tell you that they consider this operation a success.

Two divisions of United States troops, the 101st and the 82nd Airborne paratroopers and glider troopers are also under the command of the British. This Airborne operation will place us sixteen miles into what is currently German-occupied Holland at the city of Eindhoven and take us northeast to Arnhem, near the German border. It is seventy miles of narrow roads, canals, and marshes, covered by cloudy grey skies bringing rain and muddy ground. Mostly, it is a hive infested by German soldiers. I must say the people living here in Holland are some of the most courageous people in the world. They eagerly await the day they can once again be free from the hand of Hitler's empire and return to the life they once had.

On the morning of September 17, 1944, as the people in Eindhoven are going to church, they hear the sound of many airplanes. After living under a fascist government for over five years, the people of Holland are finally seeing their dreams come true on this beautiful Sunday morning. Looking to the south, they see thousands of aircraft approaching. The

327th GIR leaving Camp Ranikhet for Son, Holland.

Glider tow ropes had to be laid out very carefully to avoid tangling during takeoff. Image courtesy of https://arsof-history.org/articles/v2n1_airborne_signal_page_1.html

planes are almost overhead when the skies become alive, filling with angelic white parachutes carrying thousands of paratroopers, angels sent down from heaven.

The combined force has 1,438 C-47 transports and 321 converted RAF bombers. In a day or two, the Allied glider force will follow them, circling the area, looking for a place to land. The United States glider group has recently been rebuilt after Normandy. The Allies currently have 2,160 CG-4A Waco gliders, alongside 916 Airspeed Horsas from the British airborne. Sadly, the United States only has 2,060 glider pilots available, so none of the United States gliders has a co-pilot; instead, they pick a trooper to substitute as an unexperienced co-pilot.

It's midday on September 18, 1944, as I board my CG-4A glider. The floor of the glider is covered with ammunition, rations, first aid equipment, and all types of supplies to support the troops on the mission. There is so much stuffed into this little glider that we have to walk on the supplies. The little plane is carrying quite a bit more than it weighs. I think it has reached or surpassed its limit. The glider is launched from behind a C-47. It is attached to the aircraft by a large nylon rope. This very strong rope is constructed of 11/16-inch diameter nylon and is 300 feet long. The C-47 is a DC-3 that has been converted for military use. They are the exact same planes, but the "C" designates a cargo plane, whereas the "DC" stands for Douglas Commercial. With its two powerful Pratt and Whitney radial engines at full throttle, it begins moving over the field. As the tow plane reaches lift-off speed, the rope becomes taught to the point it looks like it will snap. In an instant, the glider, loaded with thirteen fully-equipped soldiers sitting on benches facing each other, immediately lunges forward and is at the same speed as the towing aircraft within seven seconds of lift off. The glider comes off the ground much faster than the C-47. By the time the tow plane leaves the airstrip, we can see it at about a thirty-degree angle below us. It rises to the level of our glider and begins circling until all the gliders come into formation. The gliders have a maximum speed of 150 mph but are currently cruising at about 120 mph. We cross the English Channel, and a short time later, we are over Belgium. The Germans are ready for these riders of the sky. As we approach Holland, the sky comes alive with puffs of smoke as anti-aircraft guns begin firing. The enemy is firing bombs timed to explode at our level of flight. There is so much fire coming in at this level that the explosions form a giant cloud. The shrapnel continues to hit the glider. I can see puffs of smoke quite a distance out from the glider and can hear the rattle of the shrapnel as the steel bits hit the steel frame of the glider. Out to my left, I can see the fast-flying fighter planes. As we approach the landing zone (LZ) in Holland, our pilot pulls the control that releases the tow rope. This engineless aircraft is now on a one-way trip toward the ground. The pilot maneuvers the aircraft into a complete circle, then sets up the aircraft's line of descent and chooses a place on the ground to land. What a fine time to start feeling queasy. Airsickness is no better than seasickness! As the glider quickly descends towards the earth, I can see a wire fence up ahead in our path. Of all the times to not be able to control my airsickness! There are other men around me that are sick. Again, this is my kryptonite, and I feel it's my time to join them. I pull my helmet from my head and clear my stomach. I can truly sympathize with these guys all around me dealing with airsickness. We have almost touched the ground, and I have yet to get my face out of my helmet. I empty my helmet in the back of the plane as we hit the ground. I don't have anything to wipe the inside of my helmet out with, and as I place it on my head, I can feel the leftovers as they drip down my shoulders.

Our glider gets close to the ground, but the pilot brought it in too low and must land short of the fence that is in front of him. The nose of the glider is down too far, and as we touch down, the wheels and the front of the plane are buried in the freshly plowed earth. I can feel the g-force as we land and wonder if we are going to come to a stop. I begin to think we are going to go through the windshield. With every seat belt stretched to its limit, the glider finally comes to a crushing stop. The bottom edges of the doors are buried. Our plane is now sitting at about a 30° angle with the tail high off the ground. One of the troopers gets loose from his seatbelt and quickly pushes the door open through the soil. The glider is badly damaged, but no one is injured. We manage to free ourselves from our seat belts. We waste no time exiting this beat-up aircraft. I immediately set up my machine gun on the ground. I hear a strange noise. I look up and see a glider coming in to land. Its wings are within an arm's length of my position. This pilot chooses to go over the fence. He is within a few feet of the fence when he brings the front of the plane up over the fence and down the other side. He straightens out onto the field with a three-point landing. He has enough speed to clear most of the field and allow another glider to land. We quickly move about twenty-five steps to higher ground near a farm building. I take a moment to take in the sight of the gliders as they approach and land. There is so much chaos my eyes can't take in all the action and destruction going on. My brain is painting memories to last a lifetime all within a few minutes. There is a row of trees at the end of the landing field that the glider pilots are using as a reference for coming to a stop, but there are so many gliders coming in on my right that the ones landing are crashing into the parked ones. One glider dives straight down into the ground, carrying its occupants to their death. Another glider stands with the nose down and the tail section straight up, while gliders continually come in to land.

For the next few minutes, I have a ringside seat. I hear gunfire which sounds like a .50 caliber machine gun. I look up through the broken cloud cover and see a C-47 with smoke coming from its rear. A German fighter must be behind it. I see three airmen bail out with two parachutes opening and the third one on fire. I take my eyes off the burning parachute, keeping my focus on the burning plane. It stays level on its course for a few seconds, then proceeds on a slight incline toward the earth, close to where I am. It smashes into the ground no more than forty steps in front of me. I see the propellers melt through the tail section in a cloud of fire and smoke that quickly reaches for the sky. I wish I could stay and watch this once in a lifetime scene, but this is a war, and we quickly make our way to the little city of Son, Holland. Twilight is coming upon us as we enter the south end of the town. I notice a cross standing on the east side of the road nearby. About twenty yards further east is a small windmill. I immediately set up my machine gun on the opposite side of the windmill and dig a good, deep foxhole. I am overlooking a beautiful, green pasture. I close one eye and sight the machine gun. I squeeze the trigger, dry firing to ensure I have full field cover. During the night, I hear a motorized vehicle at the opposite side of the field and the clatter of tank tracks. It never occurs to me that the noise I'm hearing is coming from German tanks. No one tells me that the enemy is at our back door about one hundred yards away, maybe much closer. They are moving very slowly. Just after daylight, everything comes alive in this place. This is my new home, Son, Holland.

Windmill and cross located in Son, Holland.

German Tiger Tank

Chapter 9
Son, Holland

Tank mine placed in the ground. Courtesy of PD-US Gov-Military

At daybreak, our engineers move into the meadow placing tank mines. British Army trucks are moving through quickly on their way to Arnhem when a German tank opens up on them, hitting a truck with Irish soldiers. The truck stops near the cross. Not thinking, I run and take a look. This is a sight no eyes should ever have to gaze upon, a mass of dead, mutilated bodies. I immediately return to my shallow trench. Suddenly, Hoffman comes running from the machine gun. He's yelling, "Mullins, get your gun, get your gun!" Parker hears this and being closer to the machine gun than I am, immediately jumps out of his foxhole and runs around the windmill to the gun. He starts firing the machine gun at the German infantry, who are attempting to move the mines ahead of the German tanks. The commander of C Company is Captain Walter L. Miller, who I believe was from Greenville, Michigan. The captain climbs onto a Sherman tank, which has stopped and is trying to zero in on the German tanks. He warns the crew about the mines that are in the field. As he speaks, a round from a German tank hits this tank, killing two crewmen and knocking Captain Miller off the back of the tank. Another Sherman drives up and stops next to this one. It also gets hit and is disabled. This is all happening so fast. Not even a minute has gone by when a third Sherman pulls up and gets hit below the turret. As all of this is happening, an anti-tank gun crew directly behind my slit trench begins blasting away, sending streaks of fire ten-feet long just a few feet above my head. As the 3-inch diameter projectiles go screaming across the field and hit the two enemy tanks, the tanks explode into balls of fire as they begin to burn. This anti-tank crew quickly attaches its gun to a jeep and takes off as fast as it showed up. The dazed crew members of the third Sherman tank are trying to shake themselves straight after taking that round from the German 88. The tank backs up, turns to its left, and heads straight for me. I have no time to get out of the trench and away from the tank's path. I duck down in my slit trench as the tank stops on top of me. I can see the tracks of this monster on both sides of my trench. I can feel and hear the noise of the big Continental R-975 radial engine just a few inches above me. With this mountain of steel sitting with its tracks on each side of my trench, I'm hoping this damaged tank doesn't explode into a ball of flames, leaving me part of the ashes. I look at my current situation and I think to myself, "Georgie, now this is a fine mess you've gotten yourself into. I don't know how you are going to get out of this one." I can only see out through a small space between the tracks when Captain Miller sees the situation I'm in. I say to him, "I'm going to get out of here." He yells under the tank to me, "Soldier, you stay where you are, don't try to get out." He runs around to the rear of the tank, and climbing up, he calls out his order to the tank crew, "Get this thing out of here. You are on top of one of my men!"

I lie flat with my forehead on my arms. I must have space, a pocket of air, so I can breathe. The tank moves neither forward nor backward. Instead, the whole tank starts to rotate, screwing around on top of me in this soft soil. After a few seconds of this, I'm worried they're going to bury me alive. The tank crew finally figures it out, and the tank jerks forward and moves on. Using all of my strength, I am able to push myself up out of the soil that has covered me. I hear Captain Miller say, "Come on, get out of there." I open my eyes to the bright daylight. I can see Captain Miller and a couple of the other men as they help me out of the dirt, shovels in hand. I'm covered with loose dirt from head to toe. I can feel it in my ears and nose. As I start to clean my dirt-covered carbine, I find I am very frustrated; while tanks were being blown up, and I was being buried

88

alive, I never got to fire one single shot.

In no time at all, we get the order to counterattack and counterattack we do. I am moving across the field firing my weapon when one of the other men catches up to me and I ask, "What happened to the German tankers?" He says, "We killed them." Surprised, I say, "You what?" He says, "They were burned pretty badly anyway." Just then a mortar shell comes in, and Parker gets hit by a piece of shrapnel. Fortunately, it didn't go through his pack and reach his skin. All the while, I'm thinking that killing the tankers is the wrong thing to do. In fact, I think killing any prisoner of war is wrong. I'm wondering how many of our men who are prisoners of war will die because of the way the two tank operators met their death. We move up onto the same road where I heard the tanks moving last night. Less than a hundred yards away, we approach a house. I run around the house to take a look. There are no enemy soldiers, but there is a large, recently constructed, covered dugout.

Disregarding the training I have been given, as well as the Normandy incident where I heard about a lieutenant stepping in front of a dugout getting riddled to pieces by a German machine gun, I pull the pin from one of my grenades. I stop to think for a second. Then with my .30 caliber carbine in one hand and a grenade in the other with the pin removed, I cautiously enter the dugout. As my eyes adjust to the dim light, I begin to see where I'm going. I can now see that before me stands not the enemy with his burp gun (a 9-mm submachine gun that fires 900 rounds per minute) ready to blow me away, but a beautiful, little Dutch girl staring up at me dressed in her native clothes, all the trimmings included down to her wooden shoes. As I become more accustomed to the lighting and seeing this little girl, I now see her mom and dad. I exit the dugout as fast as I can and place the pin back in my grenade with my sweaty hand. I'm thinking that I have just encountered a guardian angel in this little girl. She never moved a muscle, statue-like with her shining little face! I don't know why I didn't throw the grenade in the dugout instead of entering. I had every intention of doing that. If I had, I would have killed or wounded this little girl and her family. I already have enough death in my mind to keep me awake at night. I run back around the house, and as I approach the narrow farm road, I can hear the battle going on. I am amazed as I see a couple of squads of enemy soldiers a short distance away, scattering in all directions. They are running away from our troopers who are chasing them from the next field while C Company is attacking through the forest. We take a small number of casualties and wounded during this battle. Later, I hear that Sergeant Kenneth D. Witt from Union County, Ohio, gratefully received a hook up, a direct blood transfer in the field, after being shot in the chest, saving his life.

We reassemble back at the windmill, where we receive orders to get ready for yet another type of transport into the battlefield. The commanders in charge have decided to transport my platoon of machine gun squads and mortar squads via tanks. I climb up on top of one of the tanks, get settled, and find something to hold on to. This is much harder than it sounds because it's not that easy to hold onto a tank. There's really not much to hold onto. The outside of a tank is very smooth by design, helping incoming shells to ricochet off. With one hand, I grip onto the tank as best I can, while making sure I don't lose my firearm with the other. I am amazed that no one falls off the tanks.

Sherman Tank

The tanks are approaching a high bridge that doesn't look very safe for the heavy weight of these Sherman tanks. The engineers take a look and give the okay to cross the bridge. The tanks roar up in front of a row of houses. One of the tanks is blasting away at something, but I can't see what. The officer in charge speaks with some local Dutch people. They tell us the Germans were here, but they recently took off. Thank goodness! We get to walk, instead of having to crawl back on those tanks and breathe the dirt. Never again will I ever desire to take a ride on the outside of another tank. A dust storm is nothing compared with a dirt-blowing, dusty tank.

We continue on our journey. The local Dutch people are standing beside the road, giving each of us an apple or an egg. We are most appreciative. Arriving at the Wilhelmina Canal, we immediately begin to clean up a bit. My steel helmet serves as a bath basin, and I manage to get most of the dirt and dust off. While I am attempting to get clean, word comes down that the enemy has separated the British convoy by attacking and burning a number of the vehicles. I believe they only used small arms, as we never heard any fire from big guns. The platoon moves out in a hurry;

English convoy on the side of the road after being attacked.

our pace is a forced march. Parker has more or less taken over my machine gun. I'm okay with that. He is older and much stronger than I am. Although this isn't the first time I have been in combat, Parker was given much more training back in the States than I ever got. I consider him my big brother, and I am always happy to learn from his experience. I frequently relieve him from packing the machine gun. After about five miles of carrying our heavy equipment, we finally get a break.

We start digging our foxholes but barely get the ground broken when the order is given to move out. We travel as fast as we can without running until we approach a place where the Germans have knocked a hole in the British convoy. They have destroyed many vehicles, now burning on the side of the road. We are greeted by British soldiers who give us the location of the enemy. We immediately leave the highway, pass through a small grove of trees, and enter a field. We are about fifty yards away from the target the British have given us. We know exactly what to do. Every trooper takes his place on a firing line. I am at Parker's side with the belts of ammo. As soon as he empties one ammo belt, I stick the end of another fully-loaded ammo belt into the chamber of the gun. This is the first time I have seen this heavy machine gun fire without being on a tripod. Even as big and strong as Parker is, the recoil from firing this awkward weapon shoves him backwards a couple of feet. Many times, I see poor Parker's hands and arms look like they are getting twisted, not able to hold onto the gun. He has to stop firing and reestablish his grip before he can squeeze out another burst.

In no time at all, I see white handkerchiefs and hear the enemy yelling "Comrade," which is a signal of surrender in German. We take about a dozen prisoners. Some are begging, trying to show me pictures of their kindred. I have them line up. They form a line and begin to empty their pockets. This is a big mistake, but lack of training never prepared me or any of our troops for managing prisoners. No one told me we should never destroy a person's identification. We should have known this, I admit, but in the moment, I was really trying to do my best. After all, I hold no rank; I'm just a private and have no authority here. Thankfully, no one attempts to harm any of these prisoners. I rush them back to the highway and turn them over to the "Tommy's," as the British soldiers are called.

The British soldier I encounter has never seen anything as strange as this. He says, "The bloody Yanks come here and make a bloody attack. They disappear for a few minutes, and when they return, they bring with them a bloody bunch of bloody Krauts." I leave the prisoners in his trusted care and quickly get going. I have to catch up with my machine gun squad, which is moving on toward the railroad.

There is a burning Piper Cub airplane that has landed on a hedgerow. I must check this one out. It will only take me a second. As I approach, it continues to smoke and smolder. I see no sign of the pilot. I wonder what happened to him. Hopefully, he's hiding in the brush and didn't get captured by the Germans. He must have been an expert pilot to maneuver this burning plane through the trees and then land it on top of this hedgerow. A couple of hours ago, I saw a plane of this description flying close overhead of the British convoys. This crash happened very recently, in fact, within the hour. I can feel the heat and smell the smoke coming from the seat of the burned plane.

Piper Cub used by US Army.

My attention quickly turns back to what I am supposed to be doing. I leave the plane, and as I quickly catch up to my squad, I see a wounded enemy soldier lying in the intersection of two small roads. He is begging for "wasser" (water). One of the troopers with his finger on the trigger of his M1 rifle says, "Shut up you s.o.b. Kraut, or I'll blow your head off." I can see in this trooper's face that he means what he says. The wounded German gets quiet, but then, moments later, he repeats his request for water. Without thinking, I kneel down, pushing this trooper's M1 rifle barrel away and at the same time, placing my canteen of water in the wounded man's hand. The man is much older than me, probably fifty or more. He is physically in good shape for his age, minus the bullet hole in his shoulder. To this day, I don't know why I knelt down next to him and gave him a drink, but his story is also written in the stars.

I continue moving on. Visibility is very poor with trees, brush, and high grass making up the landscape, hiding deep drainage ditches. I keep thinking about a trooper a while back who was telling me and another trooper how he didn't believe in having life insurance. I just heard that the trooper who had no insurance got killed a few minutes ago when he entered a ditch nearby.

Sgt. Earnest Cummings of Shelborne Falls, Massachusetts, is walking on top of a dike. The enemy is directly across from him in ditches camouflaged by the brush, and yet not one shot gets fired at him. That's one brave fellow. You would never catch me up there on that dike, especially with the Germans nearby hiding in the ditches. I have heard the

Tech. Sgt. Ernest Cummings of C Company, 327th GIR, 101st Airborne.

Germans honor bravery. This must be an example because Sgt. Cummings is in plain sight. I am very relieved as he clears the dike unharmed.

94

The next morning, I get word about the mistakes made with the prisoners yesterday. The order that anyone destroying enemy identification will be court-martialed is heard loud and clear by me and the troops. The platoon gets back on the highway, moving north. It is late in the day when we stop. I am busy setting up a defensive position and digging my foxhole. It's getting towards evening when a Dutch girl appears on the dike riding her bicycle. She pedals by, looking unconcerned as if I wasn't there as she enters the enemy's line. A couple of days later, I hear that when our troops moved in and occupied this area, they found this young girl I had seen hanging by the neck in a barn. We also hear about the pilot of the burned Cub plane that landed on the hedgerow a couple of miles back. His name was Bill McCrae. He was captured by the Germans and a short while later, was rescued by the Americans.

The next day, we move into Veghel. We enter a large house that is unoccupied, and after securing the perimeter and interior, we rest a bit, look for some food, and post our guard. It's just after dark, my turn for guard duty. I stand post outside the back door. Tonight is one of those exceptionally dark nights. In fact, I can't see my own hand in front of my face. I hear someone walking on the gravel. I stand quietly and let the steps come near me. Then I quickly push the barrel of my gun against the person with the safety off and my finger on the trigger. In a low voice, almost a whisper, I say, "Halt." The man I have stopped also speaks in a low voice and says to me, "You guys cut it out. You are always monkeying around." I notice a German accent as he speaks, and I'm expecting a burp gun to empty into my body at any second. Again, in a whisper, I tell this man, "You will live if you do as I say. Stay up against my rifle, or you are dead." I kick the door behind me. As the door opens, one of the men says, "Hey, what's going on?" I tell him, "Take this guy in." He enters the building and I close the door. When I am relieved from guard duty, I ask my replacement what is the story on the man I collected and sent in. He tells me the man is one of our men with the artillery. He was outside looking for his blanket. That's all fine and dandy but doesn't explain his German accent. I am informed that he is a German-American paratrooper. Not too smart for a man to go out in the dark like that. He almost got himself killed looking for his stupid blanket. I lie down and try to get some rest.

95

The morning arrives sooner than later. There is no briefing, no plan outlined for us. I have no idea where the enemy lines are or if there are any. For all any of us know, there could be Germans all around here. About 25 yards from the back door lies one of our wounded soldiers. The troopers ahead of me don't stop, but I do. I ask the wounded trooper if he is okay. He never answers; he just stares at me. I need to keep up with my group, so I move on hoping he will be okay.

A German mortar round lands among the troops moving up the ditch to my right. Lieutenant George M. Lovett gets hit with a piece shrapnel in the stomach, killing him. The enemy machine gun starts firing as we approach a shallow ditch on the opposite side of a small field. We get in the ditch, and as we crawl along the machine gun bullets from the enemy are cutting the small cherry trees on the opposite side of the ditch. The leaves from the trees, along with other vegetation, are falling in front of my face as I try to dig a hole deep enough so I can set up my machine gun and return fire to the enemy. That's when we begin receiving a barrage of Stupid Fire from our own damn, deadly artillery. Sergeant Carl E. Ewell, who is my squad leader, gets really upset over this. He jumps out of his shallow foxhole, less than six feet from me and grabs his rifle. He is not using the most pleasant language speaking about the artillery men. He hastily runs to the rear. Seconds later, an artillery round hits center into his foxhole blowing dirt and shrapnel my way. I was told by another trooper this is the second time a miracle like this has happened to Sergeant Ewell.

In the past two months of combat, I have had mortar and artillery rounds fired by American troops come raining down on me and the other troops on at least three different occasions. Truth be told, I'm more afraid of dying by the hands of the American mortar and artillery squads than any German out there. I feel powerless in this situation. I cannot understand how an observer can be so stupid not to pay attention to the location of their own troops. The Douve River incident is very fresh in my mind. I know that if I were in command of the troops, and they got killed because of Stupid Fire, the person responsible for the mistake would pay the price for their error. It doesn't matter if they are a private or a general, he should be relieved from duty, thrown in the brig, charged with murder, and court-martialed. If he is aware of his actions and tries to cover up the incident, he should be thrown in jail for no less than twenty years.

I have been told by historians that some of the fiercest fighting took place in this town of Veghel. To this day, I cannot remember how I got out of this battle. My mind chooses not to remember. I'll spend the next thirty years after the war trying to forget all that I saw and experienced, and apparently, I did pretty well. Through my research, I have found we fought here for four days, completely unsupported: no tanks, no air support, just small munitions. I also found that many soldiers besides me experienced mind-blanking at Veghel and at other various points in the war. I met a guy some years ago who claimed the same thing happened to him. He can't remember one thing about Veghel or even being there. I have written what I can remember. Some of that may be my brain filling in the blanks, but I have tried to give the details of this battle the best I can. Sometimes the best thing I can do is leave sleeping giants alone. I have spent a great number of years trying to forget all that I saw and feel that no person should have to see or think about some of the things I have seen. To this day, I can't remember how we got out of range of that machine gun or ever leaving the ditch to go back into the town of Veghel.

Chapter 10
Heaven's Warriors

A German soldier loads up a Nebelwerfer (Screaming Mimi) preparing to fire.

My company and I are on the highway moving toward Nijmegen. We are near the Waalbrug bridge, a large steel bridge crossing the Waal River, which has been taken by the 82nd Airborne. The bridge has been continuously bombed by German artillery, so much so that the decision is made to not use it. The American engineers built a pontoon bridge on the downriver side which we use to cross the Waal River. It's late in the day as we cross the makeshift bridge. We reach the other side and rest until darkness moves in. In the darkness, we can hear a fierce battle going on to the northwest of us. Just as luck would have it, here comes the first Screaming Mimi of my career. That is a nickname for a Nebelwerfer mortar used by the enemy. It was designed to be a morale breaker. I know what this thing is, I just never experienced the sound or the destruction firsthand until this moment. I have never heard anything quite so scary. Imagine an elephant trumpeting as he charges at you. That's sort of how it sounds, but an elephant doesn't fly hundreds of yards through the air, shooting streaks of fire. It does, however, make craters as big as an elephant upon impact. You can hear these things for miles. Yes, they do travel that far!

We are moving west, and the enemy is letting us know that they aren't asleep. They keep dropping scattered artillery rounds, just frequently enough to keep us paying attention. Daylight begins to break as we reach the west side of a big house near the village of Dodewaard-Hein, south of Opheusden. We hear a noise downstairs in the basement. Lieutenant Robert H. Carlock says, "Who's down there?" when out in the field, the enemy answers his question with a burp gun. We waste no time digging in. My machine gun section was doubled in size back in Reading, England, but since we landed, half of the section is missing. With the machine gun set up, Parker and I have a foxhole finished within minutes. This is very loose soil and easy digging. Our ammo bearers, Avila and Henn, dig in nearby. Our squad is ready to go. Our mortar section of thirteen men is moving to the east side of the house, taking their positions, and my friend, Otis Cady, is bringing up the rear. He stops near me and drops his heavy load of mortar shells to the ground without too much care. I carry three grenades, but if I was packing up to twelve of those big mortar shells, I would handle them with a little more care. Grenade or mortar makes no difference. If either one explodes it will kill or wound us. The pack that holds these mortars for carrying is an odd-looking thing. It has a place in the back and in front for shells. A hole is cut out in the center that the bearer sticks his head through. Oh, how happy I would be to take Cady's load from him! I think about offering him a hand, but he has only a few steps more to go until he reaches his destination where he will dig his foxhole. He looks so tired, completely worn out from carrying the extra weight, never mind the fact that he's covered from head-to-toe in mud. The weather isn't bad, but the ground is muddy from recent rains. An overcast sky blocks the sun, preventing its light from shining through. The beautiful black and white cattle near my foxhole are grazing peacefully. About ten steps southwest of me is a small

Mortar vest with rounds included. A mortar vest can hold twelve rounds. One mortar weighs 3 lbs.

cornfield. Private First Class Robert Kennedy, who I believe was from New York, with his fast-firing BAR (M1918 automatic rifle) chooses to dig his foxhole at the far end of the field. The BAR with its 20-round magazine was designed to be carried by infantrymen during assaults. It weighs only sixteen pounds, making it an excellent weapon.

The Germans begin to pinpoint our location with their artillery. Parker and I smile as we notice Joseph Henn in his foxhole. It seems to us his cigarette cloud gets bigger the faster the rounds fall. About forty yards to my right, an artillery shell makes a direct hit in a foxhole, killing the two soldiers. Our company command post, CP, is in a farmhouse to my left, a couple of hundred yards away. This is C Company command post for Captain Miller and his headquarters crew. I see the CP get hit with a round. It blows the whole side out of the house. It takes no time for everyone to come out the other side and dive into the ditch. Later, I am surprised that we suffered only one casualty in this explosion at the CP. The man we lost was standing guard outside. He never left his post; he never had a chance. He stayed at his post through the barrage,

Joseph Henn of C Company, 327th GIR, 101st Airborne.

an admirable act of bravery. I am amazed anyone survived. The artillery probably came from a tank taking cover behind the trees southwest of me. As darkness closes in, so does the artillery barrage. In between the shells hitting the ground and exploding, I can hear the attacking Germans yelling and blowing their whistles as they get closer to our line. Parker says, "Mullins, you better get your head down, or you will get it blown off."

Up until this point, there is not one rifle, machine gun, mortar, or anything else firing from our line. I say to Parker, "No German is going to take me in the bottom of my foxhole!" I pull the trigger of the machine gun, and at that precise moment, it appears as if every weapon on the line begins firing.

I am concerned about the dying cattle nearby. A wounded, thousand-pound cow falling into my foxhole can put me six feet under. I look at the firing line to my right, and I see the most incredible scene. I see each and every M1 Garand with blazes of fire appearing from their muzzles. I hear the eight-round clips providing continuous fire before reloading. It sounds just like machine gun fire, but it's just the semi-automatic fire from all of the M1 Garand rifles. The muzzle blast from these rifles is the only light, other than the explosion of shells. I can't describe the pride I feel. I am fortunate enough to be surrounded by men of such distinction, especially when the enemy is trying so desperately to wipe us off the face of the earth. The Germans have some great weapons, but they do not have a rifle that comes close to matching this M1 Garand. It is my understanding that through the night C Company fired their rifles so fast and frequently that the varnish was burned off the hand guards.

The enemy keeps regrouping and attacking repeatedly, blowing their whistles, and screaming. I am busy firing my machine gun. To keep the barrel from getting too hot, I fire bursts of five or six rounds at a time. To keep the Germans from pinpointing my position, I have removed all the tracers from the machine gun belt and given them to riflemen. Tracers are bullets with a small phosphorous charge in their base. Ignited by the burning powder, the pyrotechnic composition burns very brightly, making the bullet's trajectory visible to the naked eye during daylight and during nighttime firing. This enables the shooter to make aiming corrections without observing the impact of the bullet fired and without using the sights of the weapon.

In between my machine gun fire, I hear a round coming in. In less than a second, it hits the ground in front of my gun. I can't duck down quickly enough. A piece of shrapnel hits me in the shoulder. I step back with intense burning pain from this hot piece of metal. I tell Parker, "I am hit." He asks, "How bad?" I say, "I don't know." I am a bit surprised that a piece of shrapnel is so hot. At first, it feels as if this piece of hot metal went through to my chest. I open my jacket to see if I can find blood from the shrapnel wound. In the blackness surrounding us, I can't feel any blood on my chest, so I button my jacket back up. Turning around, I tell Parker to let me have the gun so I can give them a blast or two to return the favor. I get a few rounds off before the machine gun gets sluggish, and I have to begin pulling the bolt back and firing the weapon as a single shot rifle. In the darkness, I tell Parker about our predicament. He tells me to give him the gun. I disassemble the gun from the tripod and hand it to him in the foxhole. It's so dark I can't see Parker's hands or the gun, let alone the enemy. I stand over him with my carbine, ready to take on whatever comes our way in this dark, vulnerable position. I am always amazed at my big brother, Parker. He quickly has the gun disassembled, cleared, and reassembled with no mistakes. The gun is again fully operational. I place it back into the tripod. It fires as if it was brand new.

Our 60mm mortar team is fully engaged in the action at the east end of the building to my right. On the north side of the corn patch, a German soldier tries to sneak up on me. He reaches Kennedy's foxhole and is just a few feet away when Kennedy fires his BAR and ends the German's career. At the same time, a string of about thirty tracer bullets travels straight up toward the sky, a short distance from Kennedy, adding to the confusion.

Twilight finally begins to creep up on me and these tired warriors. The fighting has been nonstop since dawn yesterday. The shelling begins to slow down, and the rifle fire is also beginning to fade. Once again, curiosity gets the best of me. I crawl out of my foxhole and quickly run through the cornfield as fast as I can. I am almost at Kennedy's position, and as I approach him, he's just staring at me with those sleepy eyes of his. He doesn't speak a word. I take my eyes off Kennedy for a minute and see the Jerry (slang for German soldier) who tried to sneak up on me. His lifeless body lies near Kennedy. He is motionless, lying dead on his back, staring at the sky with his finger on the trigger. I think to myself, I must be looking at one of the bravest or dumbest soldiers on the battlefield. I don't see how it was possible for him to run, walk, or even crawl across that muddy field, especially with all of the artillery, mortar, machine gun, and rifle fire that infested this field last night, without being killed. I look at this German soldier. He is as beardy, dirty, and muddy as I am. I'm surprised he didn't take my friend out with a Potato Masher. I would imagine this was a pretty good-looking fellow before he entered the battlefield. He is dressed in his Class A uniform, a beautiful shade of grey wool. Being a soldier in the German army is different from the American military. We would never wear a Class A uniform into battle! This brave enemy soldier failed, but most likely, had his mind on a very important goal: to silence my noisy machine gun, which he was very close to achieving.

In the large field to the southwest, I see many Germans coming toward our lines with white flags. They aren't really flags but white handkerchiefs. Our men begin taking prisoners. Suddenly, from the north, a machine gun from Company A sounds off with a few rounds. This stops the surrender process. The enemy does an about face and quickly proceeds back toward their line. There is no need for machine gun fire. I'm confused. Common sense tells me to take every prisoner that I safely can. Every prisoner we take is one less German to shoot at me tomorrow. I'm thinking that this battle is so much different from anything I have ever witnessed or experienced. Never have I seen so many Germans walking across a field taking their chances at attempting to surrender. We are the ones who are supposed to be wiped out with the enemy taking over our foxholes. I run back to my gun position and check my ammunition supply. I have only a few rounds left from the ten boxes this battle started with. For now, it is quiet. Okay, maybe not really quiet, but at least the noise from the artillery has subsided. I take a few seconds to think and assess the situation. I see no one has been killed or wounded in this little world of mine, except me with a hot piece of shrapnel in my shoulder. That's nothing in comparison to getting hit with one of those 88 shells, which will blow a man into pieces so small there isn't anything left to salvage or bury. I feel thankful to have survived this past night. I start to think about who is in control of these battles but then realize it is not my place to try to answer that question. This is one small battle the enemy tried so desperately to win last night and failed.

I think about all these young men in my weapons platoon, as well as all the brave riflemen that are around me. Without them, we would never have gotten this far. A platoon consists of up to thirty men, which is what we had when we left England. We are now down to about twenty men. Half of the machine gun section of thirteen never made it to the LZ

(Landing Zone) near Son. They must have gone down with their glider somewhere along the way. My platoon leader, 2nd Lieutenant George M. Lovett, got killed a couple of days ago near Veghel. We have lost a third of our platoon, either wounded or killed, since September the 18th when we landed. I can only imagine how many riflemen are now wounded or dead. I look out into the field in front of me and see all the cattle are no longer grazing peacefully but lie all around me dead. I think about all the starving people that could have been fed had these cattle been killed for food. Instead, the people continue to go hungry, and the cattle have gone to waste.

It feels like a lifetime has passed since I began fighting in this war, although it's only been a few months. After last night's bloody firefight, bloody for the enemy, I'm tired, but I'm functioning. According to the book *Hells Highway* written by George Kosimaki, it was estimated that two thousand rounds were dropped on the 327th in fifteen minutes of this battle. I feel strangely different this morning; last night really made a difference. I realize how fortunate we are to have come through this battle. We only lost three men, unlike the enemy. In fact, I am the only man who got injured, and I'm not in bad shape at all, except for the shrapnel. It feels really good to be the victor of this battle. I'm proud to be one of these troopers who has survived this fight. I have no appetite for food, but what I would give for just one cup of hot coffee!

I thank God for these few moments and this calm state of mind. As I stare out on this gloomy morning, surrounded by this little band of brave men, I realize that, yes, they are Heaven's Warriors, alive and scattered all around me. Occasionally, I see a couple of heads poking up from their foxholes to also take a look around. I think about what my friend, Joseph Henn, said to me a couple of days ago, "We are here to do what we can with what we have to do it with." To me, it seems as if we had everything we needed to do our jobs in this past night of combat: guns, ammunition, and above all, the most important things: guts, gumption and determination.

We are relieved by F Company on October 10, 1944. I have yet to have anyone take a look at my wounded shoulder. As we march toward our next destination, we approach an aid station. Sergeant Ewell says, "You better go get that patched." I arrive at the aid station, and as I enter, I meet the doctor whose rank is captain. I take off my jacket and show him my shoulder. He says, "Soldier, never let this happen again. When you get a wound, you are to get to an aid station immediately." I must say that I agree with the captain; an open wound can become infected if not taken care of and cost one their life. My common sense, however, tells me that even if it is a life-or-death emergency, never go looking for an aid station during an artillery barrage or any other battle, especially at night. Stay in that foxhole until the thunder from the artillery slows down, and you can see where you are going. After the captain patches me up, I get dressed and get back on the road to catch up with the rest of C Company.

We arrive about midday at an apple orchard. There are plenty of apples for us and about ten pigs varying in size running around the fenced orchard. The enemy is in the opposite field to our left, about two hundred yards away. There is a dike on our side of the field. The dike is paved with brick and serves as a road. The skeleton of a burned jeep sits on this road. It looks as if it was knocked out with a land mine. I'm thinking, "How many of our men died in that one." We stop here to bivouac and rest awhile. We stack canned rations in place around the top of the foxholes. I'm so sick of eating this garbage! I'm almost ready to begin starving myself before I eat those three pieces of potato from our rations in a can. I'm certain these potatoes didn't come out of the ground. In fact, I've never seen any potato this color! I think about the smell and taste of the potatoes that my mom would cook back home. Just a regular potato, but it was a huge part of our diet. She'd make potato soup, fried potatoes, boiled, you name it! But her potatoes had color and taste, not the grey, mushy look of these canned ones. I do a lot of bartering. I trade my cheese for a small can of ham and eggs. Sometimes I trade my ration of cigarettes for food; if not, I give them away. I just can't give these canned potatoes away. Something must be done about the food situation.

Coming from the mountains of Virginia and Kentucky, I am looked at as the hunting god. The men unanimously pick me to go kill and butcher a pig from the orchard. Their attitude changes quickly towards me when it comes to scrounging fresh food. "Mullins, can you butcher one of those pigs?" I say, "Sure, pick one". They all point to the same pig. I laugh and say, "No, that isn't the one." They are all pointing at the largest, skinniest pig in the pack. I tell them this pig has no fat on it. Most of the men, being from the big cities, probably never saw a hog before, except maybe in the butcher's cooler. Anyway, to satisfy them, I shoot the pig with my carbine, hitting him, but with his long snout, I undershoot the spot to put him away. He takes off running, squealing so loudly I know the enemy can hear him at least a half mile away. The pig runs to the end of the orchard squealing, with blood spurting out from him. He decides to make a run back to the end of the field from where he started. Parker draws his German Luger and finishes him off. We quickly recover our prize, bring him up to a small house nearby, and I skin him with my dull trench knife. What a deal! That evening, we have the most delicious pork chops for dinner! We find this pork to be a delicacy, especially after months of eating nothing but C-rations! We enjoy our meal of A-rations and are thankful for it. This is our diet for the next few days: pork, apple jelly, and graham crackers. The apple jelly came from a nearby apple jelly cannery. When we leave, there is nothing left of the pig except a small portion of its hind legs.

Immediately after shooting the pig, I notice two officers on the dike. Now I'm thinking we could be in trouble for killing a pig. We are all just so hungry. It will be more than worth getting in trouble, but we never hear a peep about this incident. Later on in life, I find that this experience has been written about from another perspective in the book *Rendezvous with Destiny* by Leonard Rapport and Arthur Northwood, Jr. According to their story there was a lieutenant who had already decided to become a career man and stay in the army. He was an anxious sort, hoping to not get any black marks on his service record. One day, while walking down the dike with his regimental commander, they came upon group of men under his charge chasing a wounded pig they had chosen for their dinner. "Look at that pig attacking your men, Lieutenant," drawled the colonel. I never knew this until many years later. I must give the colonel some thanks for creating a story to keep me out of trouble for shooting this pig.

I get another surprise, while resting in the orchard. Robert D. Risley shows up with his machine gun squad after going down in their glider on their way to Son two weeks ago. It feels good to see these men and know that not only did they catch up to us, but they are all alive!

I hear some news that I am thankful has not happened to me. The machine gun that fired into the surrendering prisoners a couple of days ago was an accident. Apparently, when these machine guns stop firing, they can be extremely hot and can start firing on their own. I'm glad I have learned to fire only a few rounds at a time. It probably has prevented my machine gun from firing when I don't want it to.

With my stomach full, I now have an opportunity to write to my mom and let her know that I'm okay and very much alive. I let her know how much I love her and miss her. I also take the time to write to my beautiful Kay, as well as my pen pal, Ruby. Ruby is my oldest brother's sister-in-law and my friend. I wish I could, but I cannot tell these people I love so dearly the truth about my current situation because I know the more they know, the more they will worry. It is also forbidden by the military for security reasons. I only tell them that I'm doing okay, which is the truth, and I know that will help them to sleep much better.

I get word that my squad and I will be manning an outpost this evening. Parker, Avila, Henn, and I will be spending the night with Sgt. Ewell in a small, 3-room farmhouse located a few miles away from the orchard across enemy lines. It's early evening as we cross a wide stream and enter the house. We use the log foot bridge, a big tree that has been felled and placed across a wide space or cavern, that has been placed across the stream to get across. We enter the house and choose a room in the back of the house that faces a large forest. This will be our viewing location. Our mission is to collect as much information as we can about the enemy: how many there are and what types of weapons they have. It looks like it's going to be a long night. We will each take a shift throughout the evening to see what passes by. My shift isn't for a few hours, so I go into the front room and try to get some rest. I'm asleep in no time. I wake up to the whispers of the other men. I quietly ask, "What's going on?" I know I have overslept. I am humbled that these men didn't wake me but let me sleep. The men very quietly begin to tell me what has happened so far this evening. Shortly after I fell asleep, at least a full section of German troops began passing by our location. It was too dark to count them all, but they were so close to the house, maybe fifteen or twenty feet away, that you could make out their shapes as they walked by the house. The men I'm with knew waking me wouldn't change the situation, so they let me go on sleeping. After hearing their story, I'm wide-awake hoping, along with my squad, that no more Germans pass by our location. In the morning, we gather our things and quickly make our way back toward the orchard. As we get to the edge of the orchard, we come to a stop. Out in the orchard to the left of us are what appear to be three Sherman tanks and three soldiers. I come to find out later that these were inflatable tanks, part of the Ghost Army meant to deceive the Germans. The Ghost Army was a United States Army tactical deception unit during World War II, officially known as the 23rd Headquarters Special Troops.

Ghost Army insignia circa 1944.

Inflatable dummy tank. U.S. National Archives NARA - 292565.jpg.

We arrive back at the orchard and spend a few days here. I spend most nights in my foxhole. The stars have decided to return, chasing the combat ghost away. I find myself gazing toward the heavens, thinking how beautiful and peaceful the sky is. This is a serious time for all the men here. We have some time to think and try to understand all that each of us has been through. We get new orders and prepare to move out of the orchard on the way to the town of Opheusden, Holland.

Chapter 11
No Man's Land

We are on the outskirts of Opheusden. The town currently belongs to no one. The Americans and the Germans continually bomb the area with artillery and mortar shells. The local Dutch people who live here have left long before the battle even started. It is my understanding the British moved them out before these two armies ever got here. I have been told that the town is deserted, although from my experience, I am sure there are a few exceptionally stubborn folks hiding out in their basements. All around me everything appears to be dead. There are no people out working the fields, only swine lying dead after stepping on shoe mines or killed from mortar or gunfire. There is no sunshine, no birds singing. I can smell and see the bombed and battered brick houses. There are no children playing in the meadows or roads, just the quiet of death. It's hard to describe the sound and sight of death all around. It's very disturbing to experience and take in all this eerie silence and destruction.

We continue our journey toward Opheusden. As we get closer to town, my machine gun squad, one rifle platoon, and our platoon leader, 1st Lieutenant Robert H. Carlock of Arizona, are on patrol. There is also a British captain, his artillery observer, and Private First Class William W. Onstott from C Company, who serves as the captain's radio operator. We are just west of Opheusden in a large drainage ditch walking toward the railroad tracks. We move quietly as we observe foxholes about fifty yards away. I believe we have caught the enemy asleep this time. It's the only way we can be this close to his position without machine guns and rifles firing on us. Parker begins firing on their position with the machine gun, along with fire from our rifles. One of the troopers runs very close to the enemy's foxholes. He throws a grenade into one of the foxholes, wounding the soldier. Instantly, white handkerchiefs appear, and the word "Comrade" is being yelled. Our troopers use the newly taken prisoners to lift the wounded out of the foxholes and rush them into the ditch, the route we have used to get here. The German 88 begins to fire on our troops without any concern for their own men whom we have taken prisoner. I turn my attention to a perfectly camouflaged dugout covered with railroad ties. A trooper moves in with his BAR and fires a burst of rounds. I step up and throw a grenade in. It explodes. I pause a few seconds, letting the smoke clear. I hear no sounds from inside. I must find out what's happening. I enter the dugout, waiting for my eyes to adjust to darkness. A couple of young German soldiers almost knock me down as they frantically run out. While the two prisoners are being taken care of outside, I am busy searching in this dim light, trying to find out what happened. Apparently, when I threw the grenade in, they used their large backpack radio to cover the grenade, blowing the radio to pieces. The enemy artillery stops because we took care of their observers, these two young soldiers and their radio that was blown to bits. As we are taking the prisoners back, we stop a few minutes and line them up. I walk in front of each German soldier, staring him in the eyes. They all have a look of relief at being captured, except one. I am certain this one is German Waffen-SS, the brutal, murderous Nazi units that perceive themselves as the "racial elite." He could be one of those the SS who are working to keep the infantry soldiers from surrendering. Being a German soldier at this point in history has to be tough. These German infantry soldiers have more than one bullet to dodge. I don't think the Allies are the only ones that would be happy to end their lives. The German SS would be equally obliging if any man attempts to surrender, and the Dutch underground will also end his life if given the chance. He also knows he doesn't stand a chance against the American soldier if he does not surrender.

We are traveling on the south side of Opheusden when we stop for a rest. I see a small brick house nearby. It has a lawn with freshly covered graves. I move quickly to the lawn and take a head count. There are thirteen Germans, five British, and three Americans. Flowers have been placed on each grave. I am most impressed with the Germans when it comes to the subject of caring for the dead; Americans must take a back seat, especially on the front lines. The Germans made no distinction between these men; they gave each a proper, respectful burial. I move quickly back on the street to join my troops. We travel along the east side of Opheusden until we arrive at a location of pre-dug foxholes. We rest a few minutes until the order is passed down to travel west on the dike overlooking the Rhine River until we find the enemy. It takes us less than a mile of walking before their machine gun opens fire, hitting two of our men in front of the column. The bullets are very close. I can hear them popping above my head. It sounds something like popcorn on a hot stove. No doubt we have found the enemy! After a brief firefight, we return to the foxholes we found earlier. I will never understand why the British captain, Pfc. Onstott, and Lieutenant Carlock did not retreat with us.

I haven't gotten into my foxhole when 1st Lieutenant Carlock shows up. The expression on his face tells me something bad has happened. He says, "I need volunteers to go back with me. We have men down and I need help." There is silence. No one volunteers, so Parker and I step forward. Parker throws the heavy machine gun on his shoulder. I take my carbine, the machine gun tripod, a box of ammunition, and the rest of my gear as we move out quickly.

Within a few minutes, I can hear the captain yelling at the top of his voice. We follow the sound, and soon we see another nightmare. A picture so disturbing, it will be burned into my brain for the rest of my life. At first, I see the English captain and hear his deep voice continuing to yell. He's lying on his back with his right leg bent at the knee, the foot blown off and the large muscle peeled loose from the bone from his foot almost to the bend of his knee. His blood is running across the road. I saw this English captain not more than an hour ago back at the railroad. To me, he looked like one of those Roman soldiers who carried a short sword. Quite the jovial man, confident with all his education and in his job as an artillery man. Now he's joining the ranks of the wounded. I hope he doesn't die. Parker immediately sets the machine gun up and is ready for action. I quickly turn my attention to Pfc. Onstott, who is in critical condition. He is about ten feet below the top of the dike that serves as the road, as well as holding the Rhine River in place. I know Onstott is near death by the color of his grey eyes, and although he is breathing, his hip has been blown away, and a piece of flesh no more than two inches in diameter is all that is left to connect his leg to his body. I immediately give him two shots of morphine. As I watch the morphine

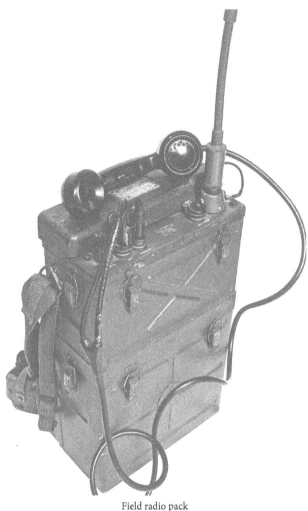
Field radio pack

take effect, I see the life force slowly begin to leave this man's body. I can't believe how cruel humans can be to each other.

I pull Onstott up to the edge of the road. I take the large radio from his back by cutting the straps to free it from his body. Lieutenant Carlock finally gets the captain settled down and quiet. With so many worries of war and now this run in with shoe mines, my mind is just not prepared for the things I am witnessing. It doesn't even occur to me that I am walking through a bed of these mines.

There is very little light now, and the Jerrys across the river decide to make a bit of noise by dropping a few rounds of artillery on our position. That doesn't help our situation. I can also see black clouds close to the ground as they roll in from the ocean. Lieutenant Carlock says, "Give me the radio." It seems as if everything is against us. When I cut the field radio from Onstott, I accidentally cut the phone cord. We are really in trouble if I don't get these wires back together so Lieutenant Carlock can call for more help. It's getting dark. I lie on the road near Lieutenant Carlock. Using my dull trench knife, as they all seem to be dull, I begin scraping each small wire, trying to match the color in the dim light. I twist the wires together as best I can, and I hand the radio to Lieutenant Carlock. I sigh a huge sigh of relief as he speaks to our company headquarters and tells them to send every available medic to us as soon as possible.

Within a few minutes, the medics arrive. I'm kneeling near Onstott when a medic approaches and tells me to step back so he can pull him onto the road. I step back up onto the road near the medic. The medic steps off the road toward Onstott to where I was just kneeling, and "BOOM," a shoe mine explodes, blowing half of his foot off, as well as blowing gravel up into his face. I was close enough that the gravel flew into my face as well. I am very close to the medic, so close I can feel the blast and the pain the medic feels as it rushes through his body. I step back to the left, and the other medics assist the injured medic. The remaining medics load Onstott onto a stretcher. Sadly, he dies a few minutes later. The other medics begin loading the captain onto another stretcher. As he is being loaded and carried away, he has enough optimism to say to us, "You bloody Yanks. I will be seeing London before you do." Yes," he says, "I will be seeing London before you." The captain is in pretty bad shape. I hear later that he survived but minus a leg and one of his eyes.

I pack the radio with me and return it to Captain Miller at the CP. It's late when I return to my foxhole. It's dark, that really black kind of dark. In my mind, it feels like it could be the Dark Ages. I'm leaning against the side of this hole in the ground thinking about many things, especially the fact that my legs are still attached to me. I have to remind myself that I am not dreaming and very lucky to be alive. I tell myself, "Stop overthinking, Georgie, yours is to do your part, it's written in the stars."

It's only a few steps to the top of the dike, then a few more across the road and down the other side to the Rhine River. At present, that is enemy territory. When I was young, I remember my family and the preacher speaking about the Valley of Death. I believe that's where I am, the Valley of Death, although I don't remember the preacher ever mentioning shoe mines. I have no fear of death, I've seen so much of it, but I do fear shoe mines, and I am trying to come to terms with it. It sure would be nice to wrap a couple of those things around the neck of the combat ghost.

The next morning, I return to the where the accident happened yesterday. While I'm walking back, I notice a German POW with the U.S. Army engineers carrying a metal detector. It appears he is showing them where the shoe mines are placed. In hindsight, my trip was just another one of the dumb things I have done. With full knowledge, I was walking into enemy territory. I am lucky I wasn't shot, but my curiosity can't help but investigate. When the shoe mine blew yesterday, the British observer's binoculars were damaged. I just had to get those binoculars! He threw the binoculars down the side of the dike because the eye pieces had been broken and covered with blood. I arrive at the dike and using a stick I had picked up earlier, retrieve the item that I so desperately wanted. It wasn't the value or the item itself but more of a token to remember this man.

Retrieved binoculars that the British observer threw down the side of the dike.

A couple days go by, and my platoon and I move east to an outpost that is in a small, fenced orchard. We are so close to the German border near Arnhem that the railroad bridge crossing the Rhine is just a few steps to the northeast of me. There is a large barn with red clay shingles that is also inside the orchard. We quickly dig our foxholes. I noticed some pigs up near the barn. I guess it's A-rations again for dinner. With the support of the platoon and the help of Sergeant Robert D. Risley, I again do what I do best. Within a short time, the platoon is once again feasting on the best pork south of the Rhine. It wasn't until many years later that my friend, Parker, informs me that during the war, we were supposed to be killing Germans, not the local livestock. My thinking is that it's too bad for the little pig, especially since I was hungry. So much livestock was killed by bombs, mortars, and rifle fire that us killing and eating a pig that probably would have been killed anyway is justifiable. In war, one must do what one must do to survive.

We move into the hay barn, not bothering anyone, just cleaning our weapons. I am making a bed out of hay, hoping to have a nice comfortable sleep, when the Jerrys across the river decide to remind us that there is a war going on. Their message for the day is rudely sent to us via a barrage of artillery that hits the roof of the barn, blowing the clay shingles to bits. I begin to think that they will never quit sliding and falling off the barn. As the artillery drops, Sergeant Ewell raises his voice over the explosions and tells the group to run to the orchard. Everyone is scrambling, running frantically as they get into their foxholes; everyone except Parker, me and a couple of the other soldiers who have enough common sense not to go outside into the open field and get blown to bits. The barrage stops as fast as it started. Sergeant Ewell approaches me. It appears he has his feathers all ruffled up. In a very loud voice he says to me, "Mullins, you disobey another order and I promise you will be facing a court-martial." I just stare at the man. I have been through so much that at this point his threat really doesn't scare me in the least. Parker comes to my defense and says to Ewell, "I know what is printed in the book, and in the case of a barrage, it says it's every man for himself." I don't know what the book has to say because I have never seen it. I didn't know there was a book to tell us this type of information. I have never been in the National Guard as Parker has.

He must have been a real bad boy before he joined up with me. I don't know what he did before he left the States, but he had done something that managed to get him busted from a staff sergeant down to a private. Believe me, hanging around me isn't going to help him get his stripes back.

Chapter 12
Camp Mourmelon

We hear a rumor that we are leaving this place and its fields of graves. On a damp November morning, we scramble to get our gear together and take a second look at the empty barn to make sure everyone has what belongs to him. The men are well-organized; no one loses anything. English trucks arrive, and we climb aboard these big, high trucks, moving out for Camp Mourmelon, France, to the south of us. The engines of these trucks sound much different this morning. It's as if they are as happy to leave this place as I am.

As the trucks roar down the highway, my mind rewinds memories I have made recently, starting about the time we were flying into Son, Holland. I remember my airsickness as I was emptying my helmet in the back of the glider. Another flashback quickly replaces that memory with the outskirts of Son, Holland. I rub my forehead and think to myself, "What a muddy trail I have travelled the last seventy-two days." I am happy to be leaving this area but very sad to be leaving each and every one of my brothers and allies that must stay on. How I wish they could come along with me. 17,000 Allied soldiers are buried throughout Holland. My mind is overwhelmed. I sway from wanting to stay here and leaving. I will always remember that some of the bravest soldiers that ever walked the face of the earth lie here eternally, never to return to their loved ones.

These large English trucks definitely don't ride as smoothly as limousines, but it sure beats walking or living in one of those foxholes. We arrive at Camp Mourmelon on November 27, 1944. I am assigned to one of the barracks, and I see they have straw mattresses for us to lie on. It's not very comfortable, but it's a million times better than the dirt in the bottom of a wet foxhole.

Since we are Americans, my company and I celebrate Thanksgiving and have a nice dinner. The Queen of England sends each soldier a small portion of rum. Everyone is enjoying the good side of life: good, hot food, a

English Leyland Retriever 'Type H" lorry brings us to Camp Mourmelon.

cup of hot coffee, a hot shower, and a dry room with a bed to sleep on.

After enjoying two weeks without being shot at, all this easy living comes to an end. On a cold, crisp morning, Staff Sergeant Glenn Travis, our platoon sergeant, enters our barracks and begins speaking, "I need to tell all of you that the Germans have broken through the lines up north. We are to be ready to go within the hour." Silence. I'm thinking, "We haven't completely cleaned all the mud off our bodies from the last seventy-two days of combat, and now here we go again." The mood in the barracks is not the jovial, relaxed one it was just moments ago. Not one man here is looking forward to going back out there.

We get ready to go, and again, typical of the military, it's hurry up and wait. We have no idea where we're going. We all wait impatiently until finally on December 18, 1944, at 9 a.m., the first of the big tractor trucks arrives. These trucks are equipped with a trailer with no cover. The weather is frosty cold and there is snow on the ground that fell last night.

CAMP MOURMELON

The 101st Airborne departing from Mourmelon.

Soldiers are placed in these open trailers as tightly as fish in a can of sardines. Everyone is standing up. The wait is what really gets to me. Finally, the last of the 380 trucks required to move the 11,000 men arrive, are loaded, and move out at 8 p.m. It is so cloudy and overcast that we can safely travel with our lights on. The night seems to drag on forever. The farther along we travel, the slower our forward movement is. Apparently, the delays are caused by the many foot troops and support equipment going in the direction we just came from. I don't understand why they are heading in the opposite direction, but I'm not the man making the decisions. The men I'm with are very tired and not too happy about our current situation. Without any sleep or rest, as well as the winter cold, they tend to have short fuses with each other. I have seen some men fall asleep against another one from being just so tired and cold, and the response shows no compassion. The cussing and bad language is way over the top, although it never gets to the point of a fight. I think that's mostly because the men are just too cold and tired to be that aggressive.

The farther we travel, the more roadblocks and retreating vehicles we witness traveling in the opposite direction. This miserable night of a hundred miles finally comes to an end as daylight sneaks back into my life. Boy, now the situation really gets interesting. We see many soldiers moving in a hurry, headed in the opposite direction from the battlefields. I am interested in what they have to say. A mobile kitchen traveling too fast for the occasion comes skidding to a stop near our vehicle. It's loaded with all sorts of army cookware and personnel who I assume are cooks. To me, they all look a bit scared. "What's cooking?" I ask one of the men. "The cooks are the only ones to get away," he replies. He tells us, "Our whole division was captured. We are the only ones to escape." As I am told this tidbit of information, I become more confused and uncomfortable about this trip. While the kitchen crew heads in the other direction, I guess my buddies and I will have to fend for ourselves, and it looks as if there is going to be some slim pickings.

Chapter 13
Bastogne

Our truck and trailer come to a stop on top of a hill and the troops get out. After being overcrowded in this truck and traveling 116 miles through the frosty, cold night, we have finally reached our destination, Flamierge, Belgium. Just below us is a small church that reminds me very much of a church back home, not so much the building but the location on the side of the hill. The company walks past the church until we come to a road just below and turn to the right onto a small gravel road heading south on a slight incline. It's late in the day, and the darkness consumes us. It's as dark as coal. We have only been on the road about twenty minutes when I begin to hear the loud noise of engines and many tanks to my left. There is no other vehicle in this frozen land that sounds like a traveling tank. The noise the tracks make as it travels is unique. I walk for at least an hour before the noise fades off into the distance in the direction we have just left. Seventy-three years later my friend, historian and writer Kevin Brooks, tells me that it was not the German armor that I heard on the road. It was the remnants of the 28th Armored Division retreating. The 28th division was just about wiped out, but it delayed the Germans. There were also elements of the 420th Field Artillery Battalion moving north as well. I'm shocked by his remarks. I have a hard time believing him. He tells me, "You must believe it because it's the truth." My company and I are only foot soldiers with small arms to take on the German army. We may have one bazooka, but lack of ammunition is a real problem. It reminds me of the biblical story of David and Goliath from thousands of years ago. Fortunately for David, he at least had rocks for his slingshot.

The elevation increases, and it begins to get colder. The dawn gives us a little light as we enter Bastogne, Belgium. I find it rather odd that I see no broken windows. We travel on a street at the edge of the town. I can see nothing but dark grey sky. I see no stars in the sky that I can use to navigate or aid me in determining the direction I'm traveling. We stop at the top of a hill. Parker and I immediately begin to dig our foxholes. The machine gun is placed in a good position to have grazing fire along the top of the hill. Ten feet in front of me is a barbed wire fence. The wire will give us a little extra protection, just in case the enemy begins to advance. As we continue to dig our foxholes, my mind drifts back home to the farm. I think about my family, and I wonder what my mom is doing, beside worrying. I know she hears the news and often wonders and prays for me to be among the living. The weather reminds me of winter days back home, although I can't remember it ever being this cold. There is no wind, and the sky is overcast with heavy dark clouds rolling in.

I finish securing the machine gun in a good position as Parker finishes digging us a deep foxhole. It's quiet. I ask Parker, "When did we last sleep?" He replies, "It's been at least two nights, maybe more." I think this quiet is beginning to get the best of me. It feels like the calm before a snowstorm. I think of the large snowstorms I experienced when I was growing up. This dark, overcast sky and the bitter cold is freezing my body. The silence is broken, and I'm brought back to reality by the sound of tank fire in the distance.

I open a K-ration, and using the empty container, I start a fire which is just enough to heat my cup of coffee. It's just so cold that one carton doesn't really get the coffee very hot, but it does warm it up a bit. I have my breakfast, consisting of a small can of mixed bacon and ham. This must be my lucky day! I can't remember the last time I got ham and not cheese! I really am not very fond of cheese.

The time moves slowly as the tank continues to fire in the valley a short distance in front of us. A lieutenant appears from behind us. I don't remember seeing him before. I feel like there's something not right about this man. He looks way too clean and rested for my comfort. He approaches and says to me and my machine gun squad, "The Germans are very close, just a short distance over the hill in front of you. You can fight it out with them or surrender. Do as you wish." He disappears as fast as he showed up. A few minutes later a trooper comes by telling us that someone is passing a rumor through the troops that we are surrounded. If the person spreading this rumor is caught, it will be a court-martial for him. This is not a threat, it's a promise. I chuckle after he leaves. I'm an Airborne trooper, we're always surrounded. Now I really begin to think about the lieutenant that just left. I'm pretty certain he was a German wearing a GI uniform. I never see this man again.

A few hours pass, and there has been no movement on either side. We are told that we are going to be moving and leaving these wonderfully deep foxholes. We load up our gear and move out, traveling to a higher elevation on the opposite side of the town of Bastogne. We stop for a few minutes, and we encounter a priest who seems to be in a hurry as he gathers up the soldiers who wish to go to mass. I have witnessed this action before. I don't know how the priest knows what's ahead for us, but somehow he knows. It's going to be nonstop action, and it won't be just the fast-walking priest!

It begins to snow with large flakes coming down. Two inches of snow are on the ground at present. The guys all assemble after mass, and we move out toward the crest of the hill. Private Robert E. Johnston from Indiana and another trooper are in front with me as we approach some small trees that surround a flat place. There is a low drop along the lower edge. A lieutenant lies motionless here in this small clearing of the woods. "He was killed a few minutes ago," says a paratrooper who is standing near him, looking very sad. He says, "He was my lieutenant, my friend."

I can see movement and hear the roar of engines in the valley, even though it is about five-hundred yards away. I have no idea what's going on. One of our Sherman tanks approaches quickly from the small field at the top of this hill. It stops at the crest with a better view of the valley. The tank crew wastes no time and begins zeroing in on the enemy. This tank concerns me because there must be numerous German tanks in the valley with their wicked 88s, also zeroing in. The Sherman is a fine tank, but it's no match for the 88mm and its crew. The 88 beats the Sherman to the draw, taking it out with one shot. I am standing with my friend, Johnston, and another man when the Sherman tank crew exits their disabled tank, running at lighting speed right past me. The Jerrys down in the valley waste no time reloading. We are the next target. I hear the sound of the 88 as the round leaves the barrel of its massive gun. This must be the largest, fastest round that has ever been fired at me! In an instant, it hits a tree nearby with an explosive force, splintering the tree to pieces. Fortunately for me, I was quick to move and get just far enough away to avoid impact. The troopers with me weren't as lucky. As soon as the round left the gun five hundred yards away, the three of us were long gone on our way to the low place at the edge of the clearing, just ten feet away. I am certain that none of our boots touched the ground as we ran to the low spot! As the round explodes, all I can see are these two big guys, Johnston and the other trooper, as they fall on top of me. They aren't as lucky as I am. I can see blood running down from Johnston's and the other man's bodies in front of my face. They are mumbling some-thing. I'm pretty sure they're praying, as I probably should be. I manage to free myself from the weight of these two men. I think I'm okay, but everything is blurry, and I'm having a hard time getting my eyes to focus. I move a few steps backward. I see Sergeant Whalen, then Parker, and a couple more troopers. They are taking cover in a small ditch near trees that are along the trail. I slowly make my way to the ditch. It's not quite dark yet, but it's close. I hear no artillery, rifle fire, machine gun fire, or explosions from tanks. It's cold and snowing heavily. I don't know how much time has passed, but there are at least eight inches of snow on the ground.

Many years later my dear friend, Karen Bauer, went to Bastogne where she wrote and sent me this poem. It really sums ups my feelings during this event:

If these trees could speak
What would they say
How they watched young men
Kneel down and pray
For their lives, for their mothers
Their wives or dying brothers?

If these trees could speak
I am sure they would weep
For the shivering young men
Huddled next to them in sleep
Or in just plain fright
Surely these trees whispered goodnight.

If these trees could speak
They could share quite a story
About innocent young men
Who died in glory
And how those who survived
Return on their knees
To honor their fallen brothers
Under the very same trees.

© Karen Bauer
December 2018

128

Snow-covered forest in Bastogne.

An ambulance arrives with a couple of medics. I'm having a hard time seeing as they help me climb into the ambulance. Through blurry eyes, I can see some wounded soldiers, men I have been with before I arrived at this God-forsaken place. It feels as if I'm living in a dream. I don't know or remember where or how these guys got wounded. As I ride along, I can hear and feel the ambulance wheels spinning, slipping, and sliding. It seems like only a few minutes, but I am certain it is longer before we stop in front of a very large building, the School of the Sisters of Notre Dame. A soldier says to me, "You get out here." It concerns me that I am the only one getting dropped off here, but I exit the truck and enter the building. It takes a moment for my eyes to adjust because there is very little light. There are a few combat soldiers with their rifles standing nearby as the wounded are being treated. The room is dim except for one corner where there is something going on. A doctor and a couple of medics are attempting to remove a bullet or shrapnel from a soldier's head. With what

129

little mind I have left to think with, I know the situation is going from bad to worse as I hear a plane overhead circling the town. By the sound of its engine, I know it's not one of ours. The room becomes even quieter. The doctor stops operating. All lights are extinguished. The expected happens. I hear the bomb make impact, hitting and blowing the side of this building out. The experience of the concussion and the full force from a bomb blast cannot be explained completely. The impact alone sucks the windowpanes out of the building. The whole building shakes, as do all the buildings nearby in the town. I can't tell you which is more devastating: the noise, the force of the explosion, or the millions of pieces of debris flying through the air. So much is happening all at the same time. The soldier being operated on has just now joined the thousands of

The School of the Sisters of Notre Dame after being bombed.

his kind living in the stars. I am saddened as someone tells me he is dead. My heart feels very heavy.

Finally, a medic checks me out. I tell him very little about myself other than the fact I haven't gone to sleep for three days and nights, although by this time I should be accustomed to having no sleep. He tells me to take two of these capsules and hands me two Blue 88s. A Blue 88 is a blue

130

pill that is a mixture of calming drugs, mainly barbiturates such as sodium amytal, being used to treat American soldiers on the battlefield who are experiencing battle fatigue. In most cases, it is used to induce sleep. Let me tell you, this little Blue 88 is some pill because I have no idea how long I slept.

An explosion awakens me midday on December 20, 1944, as bombs begin shaking the earth here in Bastogne. We are being bombed again. This bombing is more powerful than any Blue 88! A bombing of this caliber

Sister Emmanuel Didier, the Mother Superior of The School of The Sisters of Notre Dame.

is certain to wake up the devil. One of nuns, the mother superior, Sister Emmanuel, is praying in the cellar near the tabernacle when a piece of shrapnel enters the basement, passes through two walls and the tabernacle, and kills her. I am just off to the left of the tabernacle in the next room.

I have a letter written by one of the sisters describing the event through her eyes. According to the letter, Sister Emmanuel was the first civilian victim of the war from Bastogne and the only one to have died a violent death in the school which sheltered those seeking refuge, as well as taking care of the wounded.

I decide that I am well enough to help the medics here as we continue to have bombs fall. I spend my time helping with the wounded and injured. I go through a tunnel to a kitchen where I find a couple of nuns cooking Christmas dinner for the patients and the other sisters. I make myself at home as I carry food through the tunnel and deliver it to those that are hungry. I have a need to help, be it with food or anything else I can do.

Damage to the ciborium and Sister Emmanuel's sweater. Arrow points to the hole. Photo courtesy of Sœurs de Notre-Dame (Sisters of Notre Dame).

The bombing continues. Another soldier who is also helping gets hit by the kitchen door. The door blew into his face from one of the bombs that were dropped. Fortunately for me and the others that are here, the first of Patton's tanks arrive on December 26, 1944. There is a pillbox in this

Captain Charles Boggess' tank arriving in Bastogne.

location today. It serves as a memorial to a Captain Charles Boggess, who was in command of the first of Patton's tanks that arrived that day. His tank and crew fearlessly broke through the German lines encircling Bastogne, allowing desperately needed men and supplies in to continue the fight. According to an article in *Air Force Magazine*, written by Carroll V. Glines, "Without troop carrier resupply, ammunition in particular, the Battle of the Bulge would undoubtedly have turned out much differently, and McAuliffe may not have been as confident as he appeared." When the first airborne resupply missions arrived, each US artillery position was down to about 10 rounds. McAuliffe later admitted, "Had it not been for air resupply, the situation would have become worse than desperate; it would have been untenable. The U.S. lost 26 percent of the troops in a 50-ship glider tow to Bastogne on Dec. 27, 1944—the highest proportion

Pillbox memorial to Charles Boggess.

for any troop carrier mission of the war."

As soon as it is safe to travel, the wounded are evacuated. The commander of the ambulance service tells me to load up so we can leave. I tell him to go without me. I'm not going anywhere. The captain that has been doing all the operating here sends one of his orderlies to give me a message. The orderly approaches me and says, "Trooper, the captain wants to see you." I enter the doctor's quarters and give him a salute. He says to me, "I see you didn't leave with the others. I want you to come with me." I reply, "Go with you?" He says, "Yes, I want you to work in the field hospitals with me. You can keep helping me as you have been here and not return to that world of ice-cold foxholes." I pause for a second to take in the offer the doctor has just given me. My mind flashes back to the Douve River, the seventy-two days of death in bloody Holland, and then I see Parker, Lynn, Henn, and the rest of my friends that I have lived and fought beside these last few months. I see them cold, dirty, and hungry. The wear on their tired faces from combat is something that no one should visualize, and I dare not try to describe. I cannot let my big brother, Parker, and the rest of my company down by taking the easy way out. I say to the captain, "Thank you, but I cannot do that." He acknowledges my decision and shaking his head, he says, "There is a jeep waiting to return you to the lines."

I leave the building and climb onboard my ride back to the front line. The little jeep begins to make its way out of Bastogne. We travel through the snow up onto the railroad tracks. The tracks have been cut through the forest into a ravine. As we travel along the tracks, I notice that the snow is covered with black smoke. I know from past experience that a deadly battle has taken place here. At the top of the ravine, there is a flat area that has been cut out. There are many tank soldiers lying in a row. The driver stops. I climb up to the top of the bank and take a close look at these dead young men. They are all dressed in the same brown uniforms, the uniforms of our tank men. They are frozen solid, as cold as the ice and snow they lie in. Someone took the time to lay these men in this line. As I gaze down at them, I hear the doctors voice saying, "I am well aware of a much different world out there."

I get back in the jeep and continue on my journey. We travel over some really rough terrain until we approach a hillside. The driver stops, I get out, and the jeep drives away in a hurry. I see a dugout on the side of the hill and walk toward it. When I reach the dugout, a screaming Mimi is sent to welcome me back to my platoon. It comes in screaming across the battlefield. The sound of these monsters will send chills like the ghosts of hell running up your spine. The enemy must not be happy to see me.

As I enter the dugout, I see this is Captain Miller's new company command post. Captain Miller is sitting in a makeshift chair that has been carved out of the steep ground. Inside his dugout in the dim light, I see the captain. I can tell that the winds of war are taking their toll on Captain Miller. He has always spoken to me with respect. He is a very special person. I think of all the responsibility he is burdened with, the life of each man in C company. Very few people will ever understand the life that this man is living. I respect him for being who he is with such a heavy responsibility. The captain, who seemed to me to always have a trembling voice, tells a runner to show me the way to the machine gun. The runner and I arrive at a foxhole about forty yards down the hill below Captain Miller, overlooking a ravine. As I get in the foxhole, I notice that this isn't my machine gun or my gunner. I don't know the man next to me, I have never seen him before. I keep looking for Parker and the squad. I ask the gunner next to me. He replies by shrugging his shoulders. I must believe that Parker and the others are okay and manning my machine gun at an outpost nearby. It is my understanding that Risley was wounded in Bastogne so this must be his gun. Henn and Avila must be with Parker.

As I get settled in this foxhole, the guy tells me that a couple of hours ago a German half-track drove by just a few steps from where we are. I ask him which direction it was heading and if he opened fire on it. He tells me that he didn't. He says that the half-track went into the forest at the top of the hill across the canyon. He points to a location and tells me that just recently a German medic was moving out to aid a wounded comrade when our men opened fire, killing him. I ask if he was wearing the big red cross. "Yes," he said. "They were in plain sight on both sides of his helmet and on his shoulder." In my mind, I understand what goes on in this world between two enemies on the battlefield but killing a medic is the wrong thing to do. Retaliation doesn't solve anything for either side. It only makes things worse, but I can't change the past.

Before dark, we make an attack into the woods at the top the hill across the canyon. Talk about luck! The enemy has already made a run for it, leaving us with some of the nicest, ready-to-use foxholes, although it would have been nicer if they had taken the time to clear the two inches of ice that is frozen around the top edge of the foxholes, but I'm not complaining. We set up the machine gun and get comfortable for the long, cold night ahead. I'm hoping we don't freeze to death before morning. To keep my feet from freezing, I make it a point to wiggle my toes around in my boots every few minutes. I am lucky, as many of the guys are having issues from frozen feet and frostbite. I also have become, as nature will have it, an animal. When I sleep, I shiver to prevent myself from freezing to death. As long as the shivering continues to keep my blood flowing, I know I'm okay.

I make it through to the next morning. It's really cold when we move out. We are on our way down the hill when we come to a highway covered by the debris of a German convoy. This is massive destruction. The whole convoy is completely destroyed, thanks to the United States Air Force. From what I can see, the pilots of those fighter airplanes are doing a fine job destroying enemy convoys. We continue moving away from the

Bastogne area, heading south towards the Moder River, Haguenau, France. We march all day. Twilight is upon us when we come to a farm with a large barn. We stop for the night and stay inside the barn. All the men are busy picking a place to lie down for the night. I find a pile of horse manure to lie down on. I remove the frozen crust from the top. It's nice and warm inside. I level it and smooth it down a bit. I would have to say that I consider this night one of my best nights of sleep ever! Yes, I know this isn't the Waldorf Astoria Hotel, and horse manure may not have the most pleasant aroma, but what do I care, as long as I can drop off into dreamland and let this tired body and mind get some rest. This is one of my most peaceful evenings throughout the war. Not one bomb

Cpl. Lloyd C. Hood from Concordia, Kansas, a member of the 101st Airborne Division, takes time out to wash his feet. Courtesy National Archives, photo no. 111SC-199109

explodes. There is no sound of machine gun chatter, nor do I hear any sound of artillery or vehicles. I awake the next morning refreshed. I feel so good after a night's sleep without any interruption. I make a cup of coffee from my K-ration. I'm hungry, but not hungry enough to eat the cheese in my K-ration. I finish my coffee, and we are back on the road marching. I have absolutely no idea where I am or where I am going. We continue marching on without asking any questions. Another day comes to a close as the sun sets, hiding in the clouds. As the darkness consumes the light, I find myself walking into a field with large, covered bunkers. There are fruit trees in the field, most likely apple, but they are barren. I find a bunker to my liking and again, thank the enemy for preparing all these holes. I am in good company. Many horses come to meet me. They start chatting it up with me, speaking in horse talk. I find the neigh, neigh, neighing sounds wonderful, but I sure wish I knew what they are saying.

After making a bed of the extra hay that the horses haven't eaten, I crawl inside my dugout and get settled for the night. The large, covered dugout is warm as far as dugouts go in this environment and comfortable enough to get a good night's sleep. I am awakened by the neighing of horses left behind by the retreating German cavalry. Horses... it doesn't occur to me that there is a real danger of our aircraft popping out of the clouds, mistaking us for Germans and immediately taking us out. The weather is foggy and overcast. An American fighter pilot is not going to be expecting his own troops to be surrounded by German horses. If I had thought about this, I might not have dressed a couple horses up in the western style of the American horse. The guys stand by chuckling as they watch a would-be cowboy doing his thing with all the different pieces of chain, leather straps, collars and hames. I explain to the men the difference between a single tree and a double tree knot and show them how to hook this rigging to the wagon. While this free sideshow is going on, I notice out of the corner of my eye that I am being watched by all these fellows who seem to be interested in what's taking place in front of them. Back home, I know kids up to grandparents look up to cowboys. The men are all enjoying the education I am giving them when here comes a trooper, riding bareback, on one of the most beautiful white horses that I have ever seen.

Not to be outdone, I decide that now is the time to impress these troopers with a ride on a real wagon with live horses pulling it. Acting like the "Whip" (Whip is slang for a stagecoach driver), I tell everyone to throw their ammo, pack, and whatever else they have onto the wagon and then jump on as well. Everything is going just fine. The horses are well-trained and doing exactly as I tell them when, suddenly, I hear someone yelling like crazy from higher up on the mountain, "You guys turn those horses loose!" He hasn't finished screaming that sentence at me, but I know that I am in trouble again. I yell for the men to grab their bags, get going and scatter, get away from me. With lightning speed, I uncouple the horses from the wagon. I must say that no two horses ever got undressed so fast. I remove the bridle, turn each horse down the hill, hitting him in the butt with the bridle, making him leave here bucking and kicking, showing the spirit of each horse. Wow! I escaped another potential chewing out. Luckily, I never heard one word from any officer about what I had been doing.

During World War II, eighty percent of the German army was pulled and moved by horses. Over the course of the war, Nazi Germany and the Soviet Union employed more than six million horses. Horse-drawn transportation was most important for Germany, as the Germans were lacking oil as a resource. Infantry and horse-drawn artillery formed the bulk of the German Army throughout the war. Only one-fifth of the army belonged to mobile panzer and mechanized divisions. Each German infantry division employed thousands of horses and thousands of men taking care of them. Despite losses of horses to enemy action, exposure and disease, Germany maintained a steady supply of work and saddle horses until 1945.

German Army with horses stuck in the mud.

German Army with horses transporting supplies.

German Army with horses transporting artillery.

The past few weeks has been some of the toughest fighting that I or my fellow troopers will experience. This battle has been referred to as "the greatest American battle of the war" by Winston Churchill. I didn't know this at the time, but this was Hitler's last offensive battle of World War II. These were some of the coldest weather conditions we faced, with some 30 German divisions attacking battle-fatigued American troops across 85 miles of the densely wooded Ardennes Forest. In all, according to the U.S. Department of Defense, 1 million-plus Allied troops, including some 500,000 Americans, fought in the Battle of the Bulge, with approximately 19,000 soldiers killed in action, 47,500 wounded and 23,000-plus missing or captured. About 100,000 Germans were killed, wounded, or captured.

Chapter 14
Alsace-Lorraine, Haguenau, France

The men and I regroup and continue climbing up a steep hill towards the highway. A few of the guys have a disgusted look on their faces. I guess they are upset about losing the horses and wagon and having to carry their heavy loads themselves. Most of the men seem to be taking it with a smile. The men and I all had a good laugh and if only for a minute, got to forget this war. There is a highway at the top of a hill where we stop and wait until a group of 6x6 trucks arrive.

I load up onto a 6x6 truck and begin a 160-mile trip that takes a good 36 hours. The roads are very slippery, and the ice is thick. It's dangerously cold, below freezing with heavy snow coming down, on the trip to Haguenau, France, located in the Lorraine Valley in northeastern France. The people that live here speak one or both of two languages, French and German. We're fortunate that we don't run into trouble with the German -speaking population in this part of the country. The trucks come to a stop, and we climb down from the 6x6. I'm trying to get my legs and body back in working order. I can feel the stiffness from not moving in that truck, but it could also be the cold weather. We are immediately given orders to move toward the Moder River. I find a very different obstacle course than I expected. Looking down what was once a street leading from the main part of town to the Moder River, I imagine how very beautiful it must have been, especially during the summer months. There are many shade trees almost to the river, most of them now covering the road. Someone used dynamite here. During my basic training, I was trained to tie sticks of dynamite around trees about two feet above the ground to blow them apart. The purpose is to block traffic and slow the advancing army. Here is a perfect example: traffic has been blocked and travel is a real problem, especially when the trees are covered with snow. Sergeant Gobles says to me, "Mullins, take your machine gun and your new recruits and go out in front. Get a good grazing fire location and set up your outpost near the river."

I have been told that we are to relieve elements of the 42nd Infantry Division, a division that made history during World War I. We reach the river near the end of the road. My squad and I approach a house and enter. A staff sergeant is coming down the stairway. I tell him that I am here to relieve him of his machine gun position. He wastes no time telling me about all his losses of men. I say to him, "Sergeant, where is your machine gun?" He says, "Upstairs." I stop and think about this for a couple of seconds because I'm somewhat startled by his answer. I can't believe what this soldier with the rank of staff sergeant is telling me. I ask him to go fetch his weapon, which he does. I try to explain to this senior man that it has been my experience never to set up a machine gun in a house or a church steeple, especially at an outpost. If you do, you will be the first target. A round from a tank would most certainly blow this house to pieces, taking you with it. I wish him good luck as he leaves and hope he will heed my words.

I quickly throw my machine gun on my shoulder and tell these new recruits, who all seem to be much older than me, "Let's get with it." These new men have been standing nearby watching this interaction between me and this ranking staff sergeant. They follow closely behind me. We are near the river, about thirty steps from the house, placing the tripod and gun in place. I say to the new replacements, "Next, we dig a good foxhole behind the gun. We will dig this foxhole as quickly as possible, and hopefully, we can get it deep enough before those 88s begin firing."

The new troopers with me, Jack Vital, a strong-looking Italian from Detroit, Michigan, and his friend, are very interested in what I have to say about my experiences. I give the recruits the talking stick. One says, "Mullins, I have heard stories about you. I hear you came through Normandy to this place." The other says, "I have a wife and kids back home. I look forward to the end of this war and hopefully, returning home soon to my family." They are mostly inquiring about how I did this or that. I tell them, "It's been a long road from Normandy, France to this place, and I am very thankful to be alive. I must tell you there are no set rules. It's my pleasure to tell you what I know, but any of these old-timers will tell you there are no guarantees. We do the best we can with what we have. I will say that I am not lazy. I have dug many foxholes and fired as many bullets at the enemy as I possibly could in order to be where I am today."

Sometimes I wonder just how long this war is going to last. I'm not certain how I ended up being the schoolmarm but here I am, teaching recruits that came here from Mourmelon, France. Somehow their education and training are now my responsibility. In the parachute regiments, each recruit is assigned to one old-timer whose job it is to teach these inexperienced men what they need to know in a war situation. This type of buddy system must have drifted over from the parachute regiments. I ultimately wind up with two inexperienced replacements under my charge. We cut away at this snow-covered, frozen ground with just our trench shovels. The two guys who are helping me are surprised that my shovel is nothing like theirs. We quickly start digging as darkness is setting in. It's already so dark I cannot see the men that I am talking to. I can hear the men from my company at the base of the hill wasting no time digging their foxholes. I am surprised that the infantrymen that we relieve, as well as those that arrived before us, did not accomplish their task of digging foxholes. It is very important that we dig in a hurry and get underground. The Jerrys can wake up at any second, and if they do, you can expect a bombing that you have never been prepared for, let alone experienced.

This hard, frozen ground doesn't move very easily. After a few more minutes of hitting the earth with our shovels, we finally break through the foot-deep ice and frozen ground. We hear that tonight the temperature is going to drop below the cold that we experienced in Bastogne. The guys are busy digging, and I am checking on their progress by feeling with my hands. It's now so dark that we can't see the shovels that we are using or how deep we are digging. Vital says, "I noticed earlier that your shovel is not like the rest of ours." "Yes, it is very different." I tell him how I took the shovel I use back in Normandy from a dead German. The German shovel is smaller in length but has a much better blade for digging. I find the German shovel is made of much better steel with a much thinner blade, which makes it lighter to carry. It is my shovel of choice. I am happy to challenge anyone digging a foxhole. Believe it or not, there is an art to digging a hole in the ground. I let my two new companions know right away to dig from the outside of the hole inward. Never take the dirt

German shovel or e-tool. The blade is thinner but much better steel.

American shovel or e-tool. The blade folds down for storage.

from the center of the hole until you remove the dirt from the outer edge of the hole, saving the center for the last. The earth will break away much faster. I will also argue with any man who doesn't believe me when I say that the faster the rounds fall, the quicker I can dig a foxhole.

Along with my German shovel, I also carry a German P-38 that I confiscated somewhere along the trail stuck under my belt. I believe I relieved a German POW of his weapon. For me, it is a much better weapon than the U.S. issued Colt 45. Although the .45 is a powerful weapon, it has too much power for my hand. There is only one drawback to carrying a P38: if I am captured with it, the Germans will kill me.

We finish the foxhole without any water seeping in from the river. We manage to find some large timbers, and the two muscular men with me

German P-38. It uses a 9mm round.

completely cover the foxhole except for a small space behind the gun. This allows us to be comfortable while we operate the gun.

Most of the men sleep in the house whenever they are not in their foxholes, although everyone is on edge and ready to make a run for the foxhole if and when the artillery begins to fall. We don't have to wait very long. The next morning, Jerry sends us a barrage of at least six artillery rounds, hitting the house and disturbing our K-ration breakfast. The scout who guided us to this spot for an outpost explains that there is an understanding on both sides of the Moder River that if you don't fire on them, they won't fire on you. I have experienced this unspoken agreement in the past. About two hundred yards from our foxhole, we can see a German sentry at the edge of the forest. He seldom stops moving. I know that this continuous movement keeps him from freezing, but it makes some of the men nervous. The ones that know me for my accuracy with a weapon start saying, "Mullins, take him out." I reply, "It's easier said than done. It's better to honor the silent truce than to have our house torn to pieces by their artillery." Other than our foxholes, the house is the only shelter from this freezing cold. In the last few hours, the temperature has again dropped, as expected, well below the cold temperatures we experienced in Bastogne, Belgium.

It's early in the morning, and I am out on watch. I am behind my machine gun near the river. My mind drifts away from this war for a few

147

seconds. Even though I am very cold, I can see the beauty of the land-scape as it exposes itself and affords me a moment of joy. I can hear the sounds of the Moder River. I can hear the rippling of the water as it makes its way through the frozen ice with all the different colors of the rainbow forming into many shapes. The frozen, snow-covered forest is in front of me about two hundred yards from the river. The forest has long ago lost its emerald-green color, but I can see the beauty in what's left. I can imagine how this field must look when all the snow melts, and it is buried by the river. The many broken branches of the forest and the scars of war are hidden this morning by a fresh snowfall. I gaze out across this winter wonderland and enjoy the beautiful forest. The forest is fifteen miles long and at some points, five miles wide. I know better than to be deceived by all this beauty; a world of another color moves below its branches. In these sixty square miles of greenery which the Germans have chosen for protection, I have to assume they are surrounded or soon will be. The Germans chose to hide in this forest with all the equipment required to cause death and destruction. The only advice I can give them are the first words I learned to speak in this strange German language: "Komm mit deinen händen über den kopf," or for the English speaking, "Come out with your hands over your head."

I am relieved from duty in my foxhole, and now I must check out my second new home. I go back into the house, and I see that someone has been living here very recently. The house looks as if a family just left in a hurry. So many items inside are out of place. Things have been left scat-tered throughout the house. All the rooms in this house look like this. War makes people re-evaluate what they need to take with them, what is vital for survival. So many memories are lost and left behind.

As I walk through this house of an unknown family's memories, my mind immediately drifts, taking me back home. I wonder what my family is doing. I think about my mom and dad. I hope they are okay and not worried about me. I know that my younger brothers and sisters are growing, getting bigger and bigger each day. I hope I will recognize them when I finally get back home. It has been a long time since I have seen any of them. I also think about my beautiful Kay. I hope she and her family are safe. I wish I could speak to my loved ones, but I don't really write very much to anyone. I'm not allowed to speak about what I see and experience. I can only tell them that I am alive and okay.

I step back outside and go into the barn behind the house. Inside, I find two cows locked in their stalls and ten very large, white geese. The cows begin to moo, and the geese are making their honk-honk noise. In their lovely cow language, the cows tell me that they are hungry and thirsty. I give them some hay and water. It's obvious that these animals haven't had a drink in days. The poor things drink gallons of water. I check their milking status and find that they will be okay to milk, at least enough for our morning coffee. Outside our artillery guys are placing their wire for their field radio communication along the ditch and down to our out-post. Before they can finish, the enemy sees the activity and wastes no time sending their 88 explosives our way. It's our lucky day; no one gets hit. I begin milking the cows and continue taking care of their needs. I set the containers of milk outside near the house. It's so cold that in just a few minutes we have nice, cold milk to drink. I also let the geese out to get some green grass, although there's not a lot around that isn't covered by snow.

I get a day off from my foxhole, and a few of us go into the town of Haganeau. I find Parker, Avila, Henn, and the remainder of my platoon living in what was at one time a restaurant. In my mind, the building dates back many years, maybe even from medieval times. I take special note of how the building is built. This is an old, wooden building with its worn tile roof and weathered exterior. Everything about it looks hand-made. I go inside. The restaurant must have been very nice at one time, affording its clients the most in privacy, especially at the smaller tables and booths. Each table and booth on the sides of the dining room have elaborate, beautifully colored drapes that can enclose the table or booth for privacy. Looking around, I see no food or chef. I guess I'll take a raincheck on eating something. I hope that the owners decided to take a little holiday during all this turmoil, although I know better. It's February 1, 1945, and it's a great day! Yes, it's payday! Imagine payday: money in your pocket in a foreign country with no place to go and nothing to buy.

Yes, Mr. Jones, this really is the army.

I notice that Frank Taylor of Detroit, Michigan, is having fun in his leisure time. He is teaching his new German-speaking friend, a local who chose to stay behind, how to speak English. Well, not really the English language, more like the American cursing that the military is famous for. There is the right way, the wrong way, and the military way; language is no different. Apparently, this poor soul is learning the military way. Poor guy! I don't want to be around when he calls someone the words he is learning.

After spending the remainder of the day inside the restaurant, I go back to my outpost. Upon my return, I get the news from my crew that the farmer and his wife came here looking for their cows. This doesn't sit very well with the troops, especially Private Charles D. Yocum. He is an interesting fellow from Indianapolis, Indiana, who plays a bit of guitar. He doesn't have a guitar in the field, but he's our only entertainment. He left his guitar at base camp, and as much as we have all looked, we have yet to find one for him to play us a tune.

Private Charles D. Yocum

Yocum knows that if they take the cows, we lose our milk for the day. As the two people enter the barn to get their cows, Yocum decides to place a few bullets above the door of the barn with his carbine, hoping to scare them away. The farmer and his wife continue to remove their cows and don't even a flinch, show hesitation, or concern about the direct fire. Naturally, the Germans across the river, upon hearing the rifle fire and seeing a commotion, decide they must get in on the action. They send a few rounds of artillery and again, another lucky day with no one injured. The farmer and his wife manage to get away without being killed or wounded, with their cows following right behind them. The geese are long gone, thanks to Yocum trying to spin one's head off. I'm certain they are on their way downriver by now.

A week goes by without very much artillery or rifle fire coming our way. I begin to wonder what is going on. It would be nice if the war was finally coming to an end. Sadly, I know in my heart that the answer is no. I hear that the high brass, the commanders who are the men in charge, have been working diligently on an offensive operation that we will be participating in. The Germans on the north side of the river will be participating as well, they just don't know it yet.

Chapter 15
Operation Oscar

This is one of the most daring, dangerous, and strategically planned patrols that I have ever seen or participated in. We are told that C Company will be part of this raid. It has been code named Operation Oscar, and it will be a night raid. After all I have been through, I'm thinking whoever is in charge will not be satisfied until the last one of us is killed or wounded. I will fire support for the raid with my machine gun into the trees across the field. Throughout the battle, I get carried away and lose track of how frequently I am firing the gun. In the blackness of this dark night, I see the machine gun barrel; it is cherry red. To make the situation even more interesting, a .50 caliber machine gun located at the base of the hill is firing tracers no more than five feet above my head. I wish the operator would have thought to move a little to the right or left so I would be out of the line of fire. Oh, what the heck! I begin firing again. I can see tracer rounds from the .50 caliber as they occasionally hit the limbs of the poplar trees, dropping the glowing phosphorus nearby. This operation seems somewhat larger than a raid. This battle is so well-coordinated that I cease fire when our troops approach the forest. This leaves me with a big question. If the war is coming to an end, will this raid bring that end any faster? About this time, a divisional artillery drops somewhere between 500 and 600 hundred rounds on the enemy, according to the book *Rendezvous with Destiny*. I think that is considerably more than a raid would call for, but that is exactly what we do. Operation Oscar costs us the desperately needed lives of fifty-five of our troops, either wounded or dead. In my opinion, this raid was not worth the loss of fifty-five men. I doubt the loss even shaved a single second from the length of this war. I wish someone would explain to me the reason for this raid.

At their peak, the 101st Airborne had about 26,000 men. The effective strength of the 101st Airborne at the end of January 1945, is 8,968 enlisted men and 674 officers. Even with receiving constant replacements, their numbers could not keep up with the men who were wounded or killed in battle. After this battle, our numbers are considerably less.

This evening, I am chosen to take my squad to another outpost about a mile down the river, near the junction of two roads that I see have recently been traveled. The tracks embedded in the snow are a sure sign of movement. I can see they were very recently made. The moonlight reflects off the snow-covered ground. A quick look tells me that there has been an awful lot of activity here. To the side of the road, there are abandoned foxholes. The holes are too far apart, with as much as seventy -five feet between them. It could be that we are running out of men to establish a defensive line. The edge of the forest is in front of me. I assume it is swarming with Jerrys. Standing in this frozen, empty foxhole, I have never felt so alone as I do now in this quiet, snowy, godforsaken place. I think about my family, warm inside their house and Kay, sitting with her parents near a fire. I wish I was with them. It must be well below zero tonight. There are no sounds of any kind. The wind has diminished to next to nothing. I do not even hear the soft whisper of the snowflakes falling through the branches of the trees. I think of those conscientious objectors, safe and warm in their feather beds instead of in a frozen foxhole. I have to think about something else, or my temper will rise more than enough to melt the snow around me and keep me from freezing to death.

Loneliness can be a man's worst enemy, and I'm no exception. It's in these quiet times that I allow the combat ghost into my mind to play games and tricks on me. I would imagine this demon visits everyone at some point. It feeds on all the fears each one of us unconsciously allow into our minds each day. It creates the worst case situations and scenarios that could happen and plays them out in your mind. To make matters worse, I have been told that very close by, just to the south of me, there is an adjoining field that is covered with many dead American soldiers. More fuel to feed the combat ghost on this quiet night. It bothers me that I don't have enough fire power here tonight if a firefight were to begin. I begin to think that my small squad of men is here only as a decoy.

The morning breaks slowly through this frosty forest of snow-covered earth. I try to shake off this cold night of little-to-no sleep. I get my squad of men together, and we return to the house near the river. Upon our arrival, I notice that the German artillery across the river seems to be taking a break. I am truly enjoying these moments of quiet. I think the guys across the river are taking a little nap. I haven't heard a noise out of them all morning.

I eat my K-ration breakfast while I await my new set of orders. Boy, what I'd give for some pancakes or biscuits and gravy! I think about the lost cows that I have milked. I do miss taking care of the milk cows, especially milking them. My coffee just isn't the same.

Orders get passed down through the chain of command to get ready for our trip back to our home base in Mourmelon, France. I am in one of the last units leaving Alasce, France. I depart on March 1, 1945, with a truck convoy. We travel through so many towns and villages: Sarrebourg, Toul, and Chalons, France, to name just a few as we pass on our journey back to what I call home these days.

I remember the open-air ride getting here and am thankful these trucks are covered. Daylight is just breaking when we enter Sarrebourg, France. I see where a bulldozer or a tank with a dozer blade attached has cleared a road through the brick and debris, just enough for our convoys to get through. I stand up at the rear of the truck, gazing over this city with its mountains of brick, blackened from the fires. The only sign of life or movement that I can see is five short, broken-down smokestacks sticking up through this bombed-out city. To me, this is a dead city. It looks as if every person, every living thing is dead. As I am standing here holding on to this rough-riding piece of transportation, I can see the destruction: the lives and livelihood lost. I struggle, but my mind enters into the dark world of retaliation and all the dark thoughts that go with it. I can't stop thinking that, under all these pieces of brick and rubble that this city has become, the remains of thousands of people, innocent victims that wanted nothing to do with this war, lie motionless, forever forgotten.

On the March 27, 1945, I board a train for an eighteen-hour ride with the

327th Airborne from a train station just outside of Sarrebourg, France. We travel along for a while when the train comes to a stop. There is no station, but a small village is very close by with a few scattered homes that we will be staying in tonight. I get off the train, and a few of us decide to explore.

As I walk toward the homes, I notice a stream off to the side. I tell Parker, "I know it's not Friday, but it's been some time since we had any fish for dinner." Parker laughs and says, "Yeah, how do you plan on catching fish with no pole or tackle?" I tell him, "Don't worry about it, leave it to me." Parker's a great guy, but I don't think he's done much fishing. My guess is that it's about 3 p.m. as we make our way to this small stream. When we get there, I am so amazed at how clear the water is. I can actually see a school of good-sized fish swimming. I tell Parker, "Be very quiet. I don't want you startling our supper just yet." I slowly make my way to the bank, and when I reach the edge, I gently pull the pin from one of my grenades and casually toss it into the stream. Boom! I wade in and gather up about a dozen fish that I have knocked out. I have no way of really holding on to these slippery fish, so I use my helmet to keep the fish in. Boy, the things that I have put in this helmet! I climb back up the bank, stand, and drip-dry a minute. Parker and I start to walk back toward the houses. We get up onto the road, and as we are walking, a ragged man and woman are walking toward us. When they get in front of us, I pull out one of the fish and place it in my hands in front of the woman. I say, "Fish, would you like a fish?" I know I will always remember the look on this woman's face. She grabs the fish from my hands, brings it up to her face, and starts covering it with kisses. Parker and I must look pretty bad because neither one of us gets a kiss, but we can see the appreciation in this woman's face. We finish walking to the house that we are assigned to and have ourselves a wonderful fish fry for dinner. With our bellies full, we find a place to be comfortable and spend the night.

The next morning, we board back on the train to continue our journey until the train pulls into the station at the village of Mourmelon. As we disembark from the 40X8 cars which really are containers to carry 40 horses and 8 men, we are greeted by the music of the 502nd PIR band,

156

part of the 101st Airborne. What a surprise! A hospital has taken over our dear Camp Mourmelon, so instead of being assigned to the barracks, we load up onto 6X6s. We drive another 12 miles to our new home, a

camp of pyramid-type tents. I'm sure some men complained, but it's okay with me. Anything beats living in those freezing foxholes! Generally, six or eight men occupy a tent. We try to make this life as comfortable as possible, but it's not easy. The bed, which is no more than a piece of canvas stretched between two poles, is very uncomfortable. In fact,

Pyramid Tent

this bunk is a far cry from even the horse manure bed I had a while back. There is no bathing facility, so it is the old stand by, the steel helmet. Latrines are pit-style, surrounded by canvas for privacy and water is available in Lyster bags. A field mess hall has been set up in tents After months of K-rations, I consider the chow good. We spend most of the first week surrendering to rest and sleep.

Lyster bags of water.

Now that I am settled in, there are only two things that I must participate in: a ceremony in which the division will be recognized with the Presidential Distinguished Unit Citation and of course, more combat training. This is the first time in the history of the United States Army that an entire division is to be given a citation. I am proud and humbled to be a part of this great event.

157

The massed 101st Airborne Division marches onto the parade field at Camp Mourmelon, France, on 15 March 1945 to receive the Presidential Unit Citation. Hundreds of trucks were required to bring all the troops to the parade field for this event. Image courtesy of Don F. Pratt Museum-101st Airborne Division (Air Assault).

General Dwight D. Eisenhower and General Maxwell Taylor inspect the men of the 101st Airborne Division. General Eisenhower presented the division with the Presidential Citation, the first time an entire division has been so honored. In hastily prepared positions, cut off from supplies, the division heroically defended Bastogne, Belgium, against eight German divisions. Image courtesy of Don F. Pratt Museum-101st Airborne Division (Air Assault).

Chapter 16
The Chosen One

My days are filled with glider training. I get instruction on securing our equipment and the proper way to tie down loads in the glider to keep them from shifting. I also get to take a couple of free rides. We receive word of another mission, code name the Ruhr Pocket. This mission is really taking a long time to get assembled and staged, so I try to stay busy while the commanders in charge get organized so we can get on our way. There are many different missions that we hear about, but they never come to fruition. One rumor that went through the troops was a plan to attack Nazi prisoner-of-war camps. None of these missions ever happen.

March ends with the first promise of spring. April arrives none too soon, and again, I realize that this war is far from over. The 101st Airborne is alerted to prepare for the combat mission, Ruhr Pocket. On Sunday, April 1, 1945, I find myself packing and drawing ammunition. The following morning, Monday, April 2, 1945, a convoy of 10-ton trailer trucks begins moving out. We are trucked to a location near Neuss, Germany, where we offload and walk a short distance, entering the northwest side of the city. I see that just the edge of the city has been bombed, and one street has been cleared of brick and rubble, just enough so we can walk through. As I am walking, I can smell the dead corpses that lie beneath the piles of brick and rubble. A little boy is helping an old man move bricks away, most likely looking for their loved ones. The bridge lies lifeless in the river, broken into pieces. A fallen steel giant now lies here; twisted, mangled, and broken from the bombing.

The weapons platoon is assigned to stay in a house that is encircled by unexploded bombs. I think these bombs were sabotaged at the factory. I don't see any other way that so many bombs can be dropped from the sky and not detonate upon impact. I can only imagine what sort of sabotage is going on back home in the world of bomb manufacturing. The bombs lie in all sorts of positions, from laying on their side to sticking straight up and down in the earth. I am really amazed that not one of them hit the house that is located in the center of the field. I'm even more surprised at what I see inside the city. It doesn't have the scars of war, except right at the point where we entered.

I am with the 327th, C Company as we move to the west end of the destroyed bridge. We stop and everyone takes a break near the southwest side of the end of the bridge. I climb up to the approach of the bridge where two small checkpoint guardhouses are on each side of what was the highway at one time. Two young German soldiers lie dead, one at

Düsseldorf-Neuss Bridge after being destroyed.

each guardhouse. As we approach, I'm gazing at the remnants of a steel bridge that once spanned at least three hundred yards across the Rhine River to the city of Düsseldorf.

I leave the bridge and rejoin my band of brothers. Captain Miller approaches me and says, "Mullins, tie your machine gun onto the jeep." Without hesitation, I have it secured to the hood of the jeep. The jeep has no windshield, having been taken off long ago. German snipers find the glare from the windshield make it easier to target the jeep. Captain Miller says, "You have a driver and one rifleman with you." As I am tightening the ropes to the tripod, I'm wondering why the captain is choosing me and these two men for this patrol, but it's not my place to question. I am beginning to realize that this is a sacrifice situation, and this isn't the first or only time for me. I will not have Avila, Henn, Parker, or any of those riflemen with me. This is going to be me and these two troopers going it alone. I take note of the onlookers standing nearby with their young, solemn faces. Sacrifice, if that's what's in the stars, then let it be. It's just common sense to lose three soldiers rather than thirteen. I'm ready to be on my way, anxious to just get the job over with. I tell the driver, "Let's go." We begin our slow entry into the unknown, my finger on the trigger. I scan the area with the alertness of an eagle, waiting for that burst from a fast-firing German machine gun, but a different scene unfolds in front of my eyes. I notice the opening of window shades, eyes peaking and staring out; the faces of the local women, angels from heaven gazing at these young soldiers in their dirty, olive drab uniforms, wearing the strangest helmets. I now am flabbergasted to realize that this city has been liberated without a shot being fired. Apparently, before we entered this town, the enemy retreated in a hurry. My adventurous partners and I drive over every street in this city. The streets are all vacant.

We return to Captain Miller, who awaits us near the approach to the Düsseldorf-Neuss bridge, anticipating my report on any enemy activity in this city of Neuss, Germany. Thirty years later in Sparks, Nevada, I have the opportunity to be in the company of this important leader, Captain Miller. While sitting at a banquet table with Captain Miller, I drop back in time, reminiscing, "Do you remember on the outskirts of Neuss, Germany, giving young trooper Mullins an order to drive into town in a jeep?" He replies, "Yes, George, that was you being a pawn in a game of chess. I sent you there to see if there were Germans and if so, how many." "Thank you, Captain," I say, "for sending me on one of my most fearsome patrols. I am grateful that it ended up being the most peaceful patrol that I have ever been on."

Sargent Whalen approaches and says, "Mullins, take your squad and set up your machine gun under the approach to the bridge." Daylight is fading as I walk under the approach leading to the destroyed bridge. It is another one of those quiet times. There is no sound from artillery, exploding bombs, or the slightest chatter of Jerry's machine gun. The silence gets worse with each step I take. In a flash, the combat ghost takes my mind back to Holland, my wounded comrades and I among those shoe mines. The sand that I am walking on doesn't help my thinking. It's a perfect place for those shoe mines to be waiting to blow my legs to bits. It's one of those waking nightmares. I fight my fears for a few more steps and place my machine gun in its position. I breathe a sigh of relief. I am beginning to be concerned about Georgie's mental health. I sure hope I don't lose my mind creating non-existent spooks, especially when the situation starts to get rough. Our squad will man this outpost day and night, ready and waiting for the enemy until we get the order to move out. On most nights, the 101st and the 82nd Airborne send several patrols across the river, mostly to torment the enemy.

On the morning of April 5, a very large projectile hits across the street from our command post in the city of Neuss. The officials believe it to have been a railroad gun. This takes place before daylight, and I am at my outpost near my machine gun. I hear the sound of that cannon as it fires from the city of Dusseldorf, Germany, across the Rhine River. As the projectile passes over me, I think it's a mortar because it makes a sound that is tumbling, more like a mortar, whereas the railroad guns have extremely long barrels that will minimize wobble in the long-range projectile. It hits the city of Neuss with a loud explosion. Two men of the anti-tank company are killed and four are wounded. A fragment from the explosion penetrates the battalion command post, hitting Lieutenant Colonel Ray C. Allen, who loses his leg.

During the operation, patrol boats cross the Rhine at different times and locations during the night. The boats are manned by a squad or less. A squad is only six men. In addition, there are two company-sized crossings that Company C of the 327th will participate in during my stay here. The first is on the evening of April 8, 1945. I am guarding the west end of

German Railroad Gun

A Krupp K5 railway gun fires off a 255 kg round from its 21m long barrel. The projectile could reach up to a distance of 40 miles (64km).

the Düsseldorf-Neuss bridge during this operation. It is too dark to see the river, although I can hear the sound of the motors as the patrols leave the west bank of the Rhine. I wonder if there are guys out there that are unable to swim. I was fortunate enough to learn to swim as a young boy, and I would have a chance of surviving a capsized boat. On the evening of April 8, 1945, two patrols of company size, minus the 60mm mortar crews, load onto fifteen outboard patrol boats. Their mission is to capture the east end of the destroyed Neuss railroad bridge. The mission is called off and the company returns the same night. This is probably influenced by the casualties suffered by the 82 Airborne, who had crossed earlier that day. When they departed, they were 140 men strong, they returned with only 70 men. Company A from the 327th returned that same night. They killed and captured a number of enemy soldiers, including 3 civilians who were working with the enemy. Company A, 1st regiment of the 327th had an additional 17 soldiers killed and two more wounded. This accounts for the greater part of the division loses during the Ruhr operation. The allied capture of more than 300,000 German troops in the Ruhr region was a major milestone in the war, helping to bring about the surrender of Nazi Germany several weeks later.

After another of many sleepless nights, I am relieved from my machine gun position. I walk through this man-made garden of unexploded bombs to the house, where I hope to get some rest for my body and sleep for my mind. I find a slight problem achieving my desires. It appears that while I was on duty, some of the men found a schnapps distillery nearby and have uncapped a five-gallon GI water container containing German schnapps. The alcohol content is incredible. It's stronger than any Kentucky moonshine! I think it's a bit early in the day for a toast with a libation as strong as this schnapps. I can't help but remember the couple of cups of hard cider I drank back in Carentan late one evening, the first and the last drink of anything containing alcohol that I consume under combat conditions. I know too well that doing so will almost certainly give me a ticket six feet underground.

I enter the living room with all these exceptionally friendly fellows. One guy from Alabama stands up and introduces me to the merry band of men. He refers to me in his inebriated voice as "The Hot Shot Shooter." He starts rambling on and on, trying to degrade me. I let him have his say because I know it's the schnapps talking. I always felt that this man was a pretty good guy up until now. It's funny how after a few drinks, the real person comes out.

He gazes at the new .45 pistol that I was recently issued, hanging from my belt and in a loud boisterous voice, he says, "I'll bet you can't hit the target with that brand-new .45, even if it was standing directly in front of you." I say to him, "Well, now, if that is the bet, tell me what's the distance and how much money?" He replies, "One hundred and thirty-five guilders, and the distance is 25 yards." "Let's go," I say. I know of a place in back where there are man-sized targets that the Germans used during their practice. We go out back. I step off twenty-five paces and set the target up. I walk over to where "Alabama" is standing, I turn around and relax as I aim toward the target. I breathe and smoothly pull the trigger on my .45, guaranteeing I will win the 135 guilders. The bullet leaves the barrel of my weapon, hitting the silhouette dead center in the chest. "Alabama" is standing there with his mouth open. "I never saw anything like that in basic training," he says. I reply, "This isn't basic training, my friend, this is the real thing." He hands me my 135 guilders and says, "Here's your money." I return the money and I tell him, "I won't accept your money. Consider this a lesson. If you ever try to make an ass out of me in front of the men again, I promise you, you will become the silhouette!" He follows me back into the house. His attitude has changed quite a bit. He is very quiet. We enter the living room where the men are all gathered and he says to them, "If Mullins says he can hit that bridge in the far distance with his new .45, I will believe every word."

I am at my machine gun daily until we receive the word that we are leaving. We aren't told where we are going, only that we are going. We get organized, get our gear packed, and get moving. Out of the corner of my eye, I notice what's left of the 5 gallons of schnapps being placed in 1st Lt. Donald C. Scott's jeep. He is now completely in command of whatever is left of the 5 gallons of this lighter fluid called schnapps. The men sadly must say goodbye to their libation as well.

The first trucks pull out at 0900 on April 20, 1945, to take us to the train station. At 1500 that afternoon the first train loaded with men leaves. The rest of the division, including me, is soon to follow, mostly aboard the German version of the 40X8 train cars, each of which has been lightly sprayed with DDT and the floors covered in straw. Five K-rations per man are issued for the trip. Because of the damage done to the roadbeds and railways in Europe, we must travel a roundabout route through four other countries: Holland, Belgium, Luxembourg, and France. It's a long, slow trip on the train to Ludwigshafen, Germany where our journey ends. I get off the train and load my gear onto a truck DUKWs (D means 1942, U means utility amphibious, K means all-wheel drive, and W means 2 powered rear axles), the big amphibious and comfortable-to-ride-in vehicles.

DUKW Truck

Today is April 28, 1945, and according to my mom, it's the date that I was born. I celebrate my twentieth birthday with a D-Bar chocolate bar from my K-ration for cake and graham crackers for ice cream. I receive the greatest of gifts, truly a gift not only for me but also for all the people of this world, a gift from God, the end of the war. Even if today isn't the last day, I know it's getting close because with the number and consistency of enemy soldiers surrendering, we will run out of enemy soldiers in no time at all.

We advance, riding in these fancy DUKWs. They are by far the most comfortable vehicles that I have ever travelled in. DUKWs are 31-feet long and have the most wonderful ride. They are six-wheel drive vehicles, and the operator can increase or decrease tire pressure from inside the cab as he drives. They are also amphibious vehicles that have a propeller on them. They weigh 13,000 pounds and can travel 50mph on the road or 5.5 knots in the water.

With each day, the scenery and landscape changes. What doesn't change is the volume and appearance of the DPs, displaced persons. I have never seen so many DPs. Some wear dirty, worn-out striped clothes, but you can tell all the DPs from their tired, war-worn faces. I can't begin to imagine what these poor people have experienced or seen. I see many people that represent all the European countries. The one thing they all have in common, however, is that they all look as if they have travelled through hell, even though their experiences are all based on earth. Many of these DPs have recently passed through the gates of the concentration camps. If those places are not hell on earth, there can be no hell. If one of these DPs accidentally tried to smile, I think his face would crack and break into pieces. If only I had a camera, other than my mind, to catch the expressions; the sadness, the torture, and the loss that shows in their solemn, stone faces.

We pass through many small villages. There are so many different nationalities and languages all being spoken at once. I think that under any other circumstances trying to manage all these different groups would be a madhouse, but it isn't. Everyone seems to do what they need to do. I imagine many of these people, especially those from the concentration camps who have suffered so much, have reached a point where they are a bit crazy from this war, just as I am.

We keep moving through the hillsides, making our way toward

169

Berchtesgaden. I see German soldiers everywhere as we travel without participating in a battle, firing, or having a shot fired at us. This German army has lost its will; no one wants to take on our advancing army. I keep a watchful eye. It's never too late for someone on either side to change their mind. From my perspective, when this Airborne outfit isn't fighting; they are looking for a fight! I have seen the truths of this war for myself throughout the months of fighting. The abuse of so many people weighs heavily on my mind, and my heart goes out to the less fortunate ones of this war. I know I'm doing the right thing.

As we travel along toward Berchtesgaden, one of the officers in our group has been to this area before the war, tells us that these villages are for the well-to-do people with money and jewels. The villages look quite nice. I'm certain they would make nice places to live. I see all the large stones and small forests of trees. It is a great natural fortress, especially for the enemy who knows the terrain. I'm glad we don't have to fight in this terrain. It seems that with each little village we pass through, more and more Germans are surrendering. It is unbelievable seeing so many Germans surrender when, just a short time ago, they were considered the fiercest army in the world. I'm thankful for their surrender. Many more soldiers would die on both sides if the Germans do not choose to surrender and continue to fight.

Chapter 17
Berchtesgaden

The big house where I stayed while in Berchestgaden.

It's early spring when I arrive at the town of Berchtesgaden. There is an air of caution among the troops of C Company. The decision to enter the town in small groups is made. I see large white sheets draped in front of the homes as a sign of surrender and as notice to all Allied aircraft that this town has been liberated from the Nazis. I wonder what the local people of this town are thinking as these soldiers from a far-away land enter their hometown. For most people here, this is the first time they have seen an American soldier. As I look into their faces, I see they have no fear in their eyes. I can only imagine that after living through the years of Nazi control and the death and destruction caused by the Third Reich, the Americans are not feared by these people. Many years later, while speaking with a German-American citizen about my thoughts, she smiled at me and said, "George, they weren't afraid of you, they had been waiting and waiting for you and your kind for years."

We move through the center of town where there is a restaurant that will be used as a chow hall for my company. Close by the restaurant is a long stairway that leads up to a big house at the top of a hill. I am standing at the base of these very steep steps beside the soldier in charge of housing the troops. He says, "Mullins, take your platoon of men and get them situated in that house." He points up at the big house at the top of the hill. It takes a few minutes before I reach the top of the stairs. Whew! Talk about a climb. I tell you, if you have to climb a stairway like this before breakfast, you won't need any calisthenics or any other type of exercise that day. As I enter the house, I am amazed at how huge it is. I am trying to take it all in as I check out all the details of this structure and its contents. I enter a large entryway. This home must have been occupied by hunters. There is one of the most interesting sights in the entryway. As a hunter, I can truly appreciate what I am seeing. Hanging on the wall is a large collection of wild boar mounts, something that I have not had the opportunity to see until now. Some of these boar heads could scare the pants off most people just to look at them. I wouldn't have wanted to tangle with these creatures when they were alive. I imagine some of the mounts were taken from as far away as Africa. My mind flashes back to one of the muddy foxholes outside the town of Opheusden, Holland. This new environment is a completely different world. I went from sleeping in cold foxholes to a fancy, castle-like house to live in! My mind is filled with so many questions. The biggest question is how did I end up in this king's palace? I'm thinking that to be able to stay in this house is the payoff for all the cold, sleepless nights spent dreaming of the simple comforts

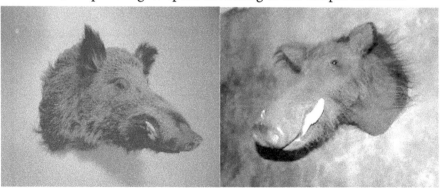

Various boar head mounts.

172

Various boar head mounts.

while freezing in those wet, dank foxholes. This new environment is more like being in a fancy hotel instead of doughboy's quarters. (Doughboy is a term for a member of the United States Army that some say was given to infantrymen during the Mexican-American War.) This place is unbelievable! Talk about getting first-class accommodations! The rooms are so spacious and luxurious. This house is the nicest home I have ever seen.

I continue to explore my new environment. The bathroom is a point of interest to me, as nature will always have its way. There is a big bathtub, including a shower and also a bidet. To an American who grew up in the backcountry, this device is very interesting. There is also an indoor sink to wash our hands. Like I said, a king's palace!

I enter the kitchen and check it out. I see a large restaurant-style stove and a large table. I go back upstairs to have a look at the bedrooms. The beds are incredible! To some people, all this luxury may not be that big a deal. I look at these big, beautiful beds and choose a bed to my liking. I am asleep before my head hits the pillow.

Shortly after daylight, the silence is broken by someone speaking outside. I decide to investigate. I step outside to find a dozen or more young Germans, part of the Hitler-Jugend or Hitler Youth, doing their marching and exercises. I think about all that Nazi propaganda, and I find it most offensive. These are young boys, maybe twelve or thirteen years old, supporting something I am fighting to end. From the look of things, they may grow up to be supermen. It looks as if they are off to a good start. Don't be fooled by their youthful strength or good looks. These guys or those of their training and beliefs have proven to be fearless on the battlefield, although the group here are very peaceful. I'm a bit confused. This group obviously doesn't understand that the end of the trail is near for Hitler and their Nazi training.

Hitler Youth (Hitler-Jugend) belt buckle. Blut und Ehre means Blood and Honor.

I meet and get acquainted with a young boy who is our neighbor. He is about the same age as the boys in this Hitler Youth group. He speaks very good English and has a deep dislike for all these Hitler Youth fellows. He tells me his opinions concerning the war. He says that if the US had stayed out of this war, Germany would have won. He also tells me that the German people do not like the Soviet soldiers because they are rapists. (Note: this conversation takes place before the Rape of Berlin.)

There is a smaller house near the house we are staying in. This young man lives there with his father who I see through the window. He is an artist, busy at his work, looking in the distance at the far-off landscape of the Alps. I knock on the door, and he asks me to enter. He too speaks very good English. I ask him if he would do a painting of me. He says he'd be more than happy to and gives me an appointment. The next day I arrive and spend two hours sitting as he begins my portrait. This goes on for two hours a day for sixteen days. While he is busy doing his painting, I talk to him and have the opportunity to ask a few questions. He tells me he has served in many battles, most recently serving as the commander of an anti-aircraft battery. I ask him about Hitler. He says he saw Hitler here in Berchtesgaden two years ago, and he was kaput, stooped over and in bad health. He also tells me that in 1939, he attended the New York World's Fair where he won a blue ribbon for one of his paintings. It was a painting of the beautiful, scenic mountains of the Berchtesgaden Alps. When he finishes my portrait, he autographs the painting for me, signing his name, Wurm. I pay him a very small amount for the hours of work that he has invested in my painting. I give him my last K-ration and thirty-five marks. It would have made me happy if I had more to give him, especially food, but sadly, I did not have the food or more money to give him. He was very happy to receive what I gave him, and with a friendly exchange of danke schön (thank-you), I return to the house with my painting. I think he did an excellent job! I show the portrait to Yocum and Parker, who also get their portraits done. He also did photography work, taking professional photographs. I am fortunate enough to have a few of them.

Sitting in this big, old house causes my mind to start drifting off, and I find myself thinking about an entirely different subject, my appetite. Seems it increases with each day that passes. Those five K-rations that I was issued days ago are long gone. Believe me, it's slim pickings, but we are better off than the local people. What little food we are given at the company chow hall is not enough to fill a man's stomach. For breakfast, we have a cup of coffee and one spoon full of a C-ration. One of the men

This is a re-creation by Janet Young, a local artist in Redway, California, done from a photograpgh of the original.

found some flour and apples to make apple pies for lunch. For lunch, we have a piece of apple pie and a cup of coffee, and for the last meal of the day, we have the same as breakfast, again just one spoon full of C-ration and a cup of coffee. This goes on for many days until supplies reach us.

I finish my four-hour shift of guard duty, and I prepare to go find some real food. It is just me and another trooper from my platoon who enjoys the mountain travel on this climbing expedition. I toss my rifle on my shoulder and begin my hike into the rough alpine mountains to see if I can find something to eat. I think about killing a cow, but I back away from this idea because I am certain that what few head of cattle are here are owned by the local farmers who probably need these animals more than I do. I know that I wouldn't be too happy if some stranger came and killed one of my family's cows, so I continue my search. I reach the crest of a hill after hiking up through a canyon. These snow-capped mountains must be the most beautiful mountains that were ever created! It is paradise for this mountain boy. I see smoke rising from a cliff of rocks and forest. We follow a trail and begin our approach to where the smoke is coming from. We casually walk into a camp of German soldiers dressed in their grey uniforms. They are busy stacking and burning their rifles. The past couple of nights have been cold, and they are wearing their long wool coats as they wait for the temperature to drop when the sun goes down. Instead of wearing their steel helmets, they are all wearing their warm wool caps. We join the group of Germans to watch as they hastily burn a stack of beautiful rifles. It is so quiet. In fact, this is the quietest bunch of soldiers that I have ever encountered. I see sadness in their faces. I would be sad, too, if I had to stand by watching my rifle burn. Then I think about being on the other side of the fence. As recently as yesterday, along with so many other yesterdays, I have seen so many faces of the abused people that have been classified as DPs. The trooper and I leave the group of Germans. We walk up the canyon a short distance. We stop and turn to view these men, the soldiers of yesterday. They slowly fade away, becoming part of the trail through the forest, leaving their legacy in the smoke of their burning rifles, along with their active roles during the past five years of death and destruction.

It's early May, and I am very happy. Spring has finally sprung into full glory,

177

and I am enjoying my personal mission of exploration in this beautiful forest. There are freshwater streams and many mountains of stone. We find two young German infantry soldiers lying dead near a small campsite. It appears that they were recently killed, not by our troops, but from the looks of things, there is no doubt these two were killed by the German SS. As the war comes to an end, the SS are so afraid of paying for their war crimes that they are killing their own German infantry troops, taking their identification, then passing through our troops as German infantry.

A young lady comes into town reporting that there is an SS officer hiding at her home. With so many of the local people coming to us to report these SS men in hiding, we don't ever have to go look for them. Our company commander, Captain Clifford J. Bolander from Youngstown, Ohio, sends a lieutenant, a driver, and one-armed rifleman to escort her. Upon entering the home, her father points to a stairway, stating that he is up there, you can find him in bed. No time is wasted by the patrol pulling the SS man out of bed and downstairs. The house explodes with the anger from this young woman towards this officer. She is trying her best to kill this Nazi, using only her hands. The patrol has to contain the woman. They overpower her and restrain her. It is my understanding that the SS man came into her home, killing her brother. Then, after taking his identity papers, had the guts to go upstairs and go to bed. The lieutenant delivers him to headquarters. I never see him again or hear what became of him. I am beginning to realize that the SS are not very popular among the people of this community. I find it very hard to believe that these Nazis would kill their own people to save their hides. If ever I wanted to use my hunting skills to hunt down a human, it would be these SS Nazis.

One of my explorer friends and I are hiking and exploring around the area. We come to a large shop, where we can hear a commotion coming from inside. As I open the door, a group of people begin to gather around me and my friend, swarming around us like a swarm of honeybees in a field of flowers. Everyone is asking, "Sprechen Sie Deutsch?" The confusion settles down a bit as I realize what is going on. There is an older guy standing on a makeshift stage. I have to imagine that he is SS by the way these folks treat him. With so many people talking at the same time, not one of them looks or acts like they are very happy. I climb onto the stage and do my usual routine, checking for guns and other paraphernalia. I'm not using the nicest language, but this is the military language that I have become accustomed to using. I begin to search this man for contraband. He is a strange one. He carries no loot or weapons, not even a small .32 caliber pistol. The German officers were infamous for keeping one of these personal weapons in their pocket. I guess it's going to be slim pickings for this Eagle today. After checking him for weapons, I take him to battalion headquarters. A 1st lieutenant appears from another room. He looks at this German SS guy and gives him an order in such a strong, powerful voice that it startles me. He tells the man to strip down. The guy wastes no time getting his clothes off until he is down to his birthday suit. This is the first and only prisoner to pull the wool over my eyes. I stand there in amazement as I watch him quickly undress. As the man drops his trousers, a huge cache of loot falls out of his bloused pants. I can't believe I overlooked this much when I shook him down. He had it all hidden in his bloused pants! Expensive watches, gold rings, and all sorts of items of value. Sadly for him, none of these items will matter where he is going. He won't need any of these things. The lieutenant tells me he had the SS tattoo under his left arm, but I didn't see it. I leave this prisoner in the lieutenant's care, walk back toward my fancy home, and begin climbing up the steps leading to the house.

On May 8, 1945, we are informed that the war is over, but V-E Day (Victory in Europe) is nothing more than another day for me. The race continues to catch the big wigs of the German Army. What rewards await the trooper that brings in the number one Nazi, Adolph Hitler? The thought of capturing and bringing in the Führer is enough excitement for any man in Company C, and this is now the top priority for these troopers, along with the rest of the world. I am fortunate enough to be the sergeant of the guard at Berchestgaden Hoff Hotel at this time when most of the top brass and officers of the Third Reich in this area are being rounded up.

There are captures taking place regularly. The first capture goes to the 36th Division, who get the second most important Nazi in Germany. Reichsmarshall Hermann Göring, Deputy Führer and chief of Germany's Luftwaffe, was taken prisoner on May 9, 1945, one day after V-E Day in the village of Schleching, Bavaria, on a road near Salzburg, following negotiations between his personal adjutant and 36th Division officers. His wife and daughter are in his company when they are captured.

Erich Kempka was Hitler's chauffeur. He is captured and claims to have seen the burned bodies of Hitler and Ava Braun in a bunker 55 feet under the Reich Chancellory before escaping to Berchestgaden. There are many more captures taking place daily as the quest for the top-ranking German military is carried out.

Hitler in his Mercedes being driven through Berchtesgaden by his driver, Eric Kempka.

BERCHTESGADEN

There are many treasures that are also being confiscated and loaded up on trucks by the 327th. Over four million dollars in 26 different currencies, as well as various pieces of art that are collected, cataloged, and loaded. Thirteen wagon loads come from just one of the many salt mines that were used to store all the loot that was stolen. One of the most interesting finds as noted in *Rendezvous with Destiny* comes from Hitler's personal physician, Dr. Morell's home, where a 100,000x microscope is recovered. It weighs 22 tons. Over 80 wagon loads of art and cultural objects from across Europe are found in the salt mines, including what the Germans thought was Da Vinci's Mona Lisa. When the painting was returned, it is confirmed that it is a copy, not the original.

Members of the 327th unloading Hermann Göring's looted art treasures at Unerstein, just outside of Berchetesgaden.

A trooper from the 101st Airborne looks over many gold objects plundered by the Nazis. Courtesy of South Denver VFW Post 2461.

These are a few of the thousands of wedding rings the Germans removed from their victims in order to salvage the gold. U.S. First Army troops found these rings, along with watches, precious stones, eyeglasses, and gold teeth fillings, in a cave adjoining the Buchenwald concentration camp near Weimar, Germany. May 5, 1945.

I take a ride with a lieutenant in his jeep. We load troopers in the jeep until we exceed the capacity of this vehicle. We are traveling on a mountain highway leading out of Germany into Austria. Yes, it's a bit uncomfortable since we have too many passengers. I decide that there is an easy way to take care of this problem. We meet a convoy commanded by a German officer. We stop the convoy and climb out of our jeep. The lieutenant can speak a bit of German, and he tells the officer in charge of the convoy that we need his vehicle. The German is told to go back and ride with the people in the convoy. He tries desperately to persuade the lieutenant by reaching in his briefcase for proof not to take his jeep because he has permission from Americans to deliver the convoy. The German officer doesn't take his eyes off me as he takes his paperwork and steps out of his jeep, saying, "What a pity," as we leave their convoy minus a jeep.

I am very proud of my jeep, although how I acquired it is something that I'm not proud of. I should have honored this German's paperwork that was signed by American officials. The people traveling with this German officer that I took the jeep from were dressed in civilian clothes and quite possibly could be important people, maybe scientists that were employed by Hitler's Nazi regime. This jeep and the American jeep are the vehicles I learn how to drive in. This will be my transportation for the coming days in and around Berchtesgaden.

The Screaming Eagles capture one of the big prizes as a second important Nazi is caught by the 101st

My two little jeeps I learned to drive in, a German Kubelwagon and a U.S. Willy's Jeep.

Airborne. Doctor Robert Ley is a giant catch. He is the treasurer of the Nazi Party. Doctor Ley is also the leader of the Nazi Labor Front and the Strength through Joy movement. On May 16, 1945, he is captured by A Company of the 506th, PIR in a shoemaker's house. These roundups last a week or more. A number of the German high-ranking officials, including those SS in their black uniforms with the iron cross hanging from their necks are brought in to be processed. Many of these men that were picked to do Hitler's dirty work are being rounded up and brought into the Hotel Berchtesgaden Haus Hohendal. I spend many hours at the hotel as sergeant of the guard. Of all these important Nazis that I am guarding, I come to know only one of them, Joachim Von Ribbentrop. He was

Hotel Berchtesgaden Haus Hohendal

the Foreign Minister of Nazi Germany. I find him to be a very nervous sort of guy. He continually paces across the porch of the hotel in his dress uniform. I suppose if my future was as bleak as his, I too would be pacing back and forth. I can't begin to imagine what goes through a man's mind when he knows that he now must pay the price for his crimes. He was eventually tried and convicted for crimes against peace, deliberately planning a war of aggression, war crimes, and crimes against humanity. He

Joachim Von Ribbontrop

was hanged on October 16, 1946. Ultimately, 13 men are tried and hung at the Nuremberg Trials. The only two men who escaped hanging were Hermann Göring and Robert Ley, who both committed suicide.

I use my jeep to transport men to the various posts we guard. I have no trouble posting the guard with the guys that trust my driving, but some of them choose to walk. Hey, I'm just learning! I drive my jeep on a road that leads up the mountain to the Eagle's Nest (Kehlsteinhaus). It has recently been paved and is the most incredible road, especially considering its location. The terrain here makes it look impossible to construct a roadway in these mountains. Many of the men are interested in der Führer's hangout, the Eagle's Nest, but I don't care. I am interested in what lies beyond the entrance of the salt mine that my men and I are guarding, its entrance located about halfway to the Eagles Nest from the bottom of the mountain. A couple of troopers and I decide to take a look inside. Using only a kerosene lantern for light, we travel on a walkway that is on the side of the cave. We find a storage room filled with the plunder of the German war mongers: valuables and heirlooms taken from families, many of whom were killed by the Nazi's, precious, holy things from churches and synagogues, art from homes and museums, now all organized and stored in one place.

I pick a butcher knife to have as a memento of this place. Why? I don't know. Maybe it was from having to use my trench knife to butcher those pigs, which was no easy task. In my youthful haste, I have managed to cut my leg with the sharp butcher knife. Of all the places I could be, here I am in a cave without sufficient light, and of course, I left my first aid packet back with my pack. With the help of my two friends and using what little light we have, we manage to slow the bleeding. I bandage my leg the best I can, using a piece of cloth from the pile of loot. Then we find our way back out of the salt mine. I return to the big house without going to the aid station. I can hear the captain who looked at my shoulder a while back, saying always get to the aid station, but my stubborn mind will have none of that. As I'm getting into bed, I'm thinking everything is ok. I wake up later in the night feeling very weak. I check my wound. It hasn't stopped bleeding. It has been bleeding far too long now. I take extra care bandaging the wound this time, stopping the bleeding. I stay awake until daybreak. I know that I have lost far too much blood, and I don't want to bleed to death in my sleep. At dawn, I check the wound. It has not started bleeding and is looking okay. Another dangerous lesson that I have learned the hard way.

During my stay in Berchtesgaden, 1st Sgt. Goble makes a decision that is very much to my liking. He promotes both Parker and me to buck sergeant. It is my understanding that there was a sergeant's meeting where the sergeants got together to decide who would be promoted and join the ranks of the sergeants. As the story was relayed to me, Sergeant Goble was the one that spoke up at the meeting. They had discussed who would be the men they would promote. Sergeant Goble stood up and said, "Wait a minute. What about the damn kid? He's been with the unit since day one of this mess and has survived every man we have promoted in the field. I'm tired of replacing men over him, so he's got to be promoted. He's the man we should give the stripes to." With my new-found promotion, I decide to get these men or keep these men in the weapons platoon in shape. I begin an exercise regime for the platoon, calisthenics mostly, and a bit of close order drill. I guess the men don't mind. At least, I never hear any back talk or complaints.

I am relieved from my shift of guard duty and have made my way back to the big house, when one of my explorer friends, returning from the day's adventure, approaches me. I ask, "Where have you travelled today?" He responds, "Dachau." Dachau was the first Nazi concentration camp. It was built in 1933 to house political prisoners. As the war continued, it also held forced labor and a large number of Jews. Its occupants lived in constant fear of brutal treatment and death. There were over 32,000 documented deaths at this camp and countless undocumented deaths. It operated until April 29, 1945. It was a convenient location, as the Nazi's had their official headquarters in Munich, Germany. Dachau is about 100 miles north of Berchestgaden and about 30 miles north of Munich. I ask, "What did you see there?" He responds, "I saw the conveyor they used to move the remains of burned bodies. It hasn't been cleaned. It is covered with bones and debris from its last use." I can only imagine what this man has seen. This is a place I never want to see. He says to me, "Are you going to go and take a look?" I pause for a few minutes, while I continue processing the images my mind is creating. "No" I say, "I think I will pass, as I have seen more than enough death in the past two years to keep me awake the rest of my life."

Later in the day, I am talking with Parker. He has some sad news to give me. It appears that my friend, Otis Cady, was KIA. Apparently back in Bastogne, he was bringing some prisoners to the rear. They were near a barn when the Germans began shelling, killing both the prisoners and Cady. I know the Sky Pilot is flying high now watching over us.

A few days later here in Berchestgaden, Parker and I are fortunate enough to be promoted again, making both of us staff sergeants. I'm feeling pretty good about my promotion. I currently am filling the role of

The Unknown Inmate by Fritz Koelle, erected in 1950 north of the old crematorium. The caption translates to read, "To honor the dead, to remind the living."

tech sergeant, so it's nice that I get this promotion, again with the help and support of 1st Sergeant Goble. Thanks to his kind words, I am now Staff Sergeant Mullins. Probably the only man around who went from a private with no stripes to a staff sergeant with three up and one down within a week! I hope I can live up to the challenge. For the next eight months before returning home, I have all the responsibility of but never received the rating of tech sergeant.

Parker and a few of the other troopers are high point men, which means they are first to leave for home, based on the point system. I am happy to see them on their way home, but for me, it is also a sad time. After being through all the atrocities of war with these men, the time has come for us to part ways. We shake hands and say goodbye for the last time on foreign soil. I will be in the next group to leave. I am one of the second high point men, although the way the army works, who knows when that will be. I know I will be leaving Berchtesgaden soon.

For many days, the town of Berchtesgaden is a busy place. I am standing near a trooper in Berchestgaden and ask him, "What's all the fuss about?" He then tells me about the worst case of rape that I have ever heard of or will ever hear of again. It, sadly, was committed by one of our GIs. I understand that he was being tried by the law of the land of Germany at the time. Capital punishment means the gallows here. I hope he is not from my regiment. I have made lots of good memories here, also some bad ones. I have tried to tell many of my good memories, but I do not choose to attempt to tell all the details that were told to me about my worst memory, this horrifying case of rape. It is sad for me to think that a person who wears the same uniform as me has committed such a horrendous crime. I have found no report or record of this incident anywhere, and I am not willing to relay all the disgusting details of this case.

As we get comfortable living here in Berchestgaden, the troops and I find ourselves with many hours of free time to pursue our other interests. Being something of an outdoorsman, I spend my free time exploring and investigating the beautiful countryside. Some of the men spend their time playing cards and dice or participating in all types of sports, including boxing, mountain climbing, you name it. Some of the troops go horseback riding on their off-hours, Horseback riding can be enjoyable, but I have spent a fair share of my time as a young boy getting bucked and thrown around while breaking horses with my dad, so I decide it's probably best for me to just watch from afar. Mostly we try to keep minds occupied while we wait for orders to go home.

Cpl. Walker Pugh of the 101st Airborne, 327th GIR, D Company
rides a horse in the streets of Berchestgaden.

Some of the boys and I are enjoying the peace and quiet of Berchtesgaden.

Chapter 18
Bischoffen, Austria

I am awaiting our only inspection in Bishchoffen in my Class
A uniform.

Up to this point, my life has been so full of many wonderful experiences and some not so wonderful. I'm especially happy about being in Berchestgaden. In fact, I'm starting to feel at home here. Unfortunately, it's time to leave. It is with mixed feelings that I get ready to go. We get packed like sardines into 6x6s, and with a touch of sadness, I think about the new toy I am leaving behind: my little jeep, parked out back. Hopefully, it will go back to its rightful owner.

The truck engine roars, puffing out black smoke, and we are on our way over the mountain, 12 miles to Bischoffen, Austria. We arrive in another beautiful valley with mountains as steep as a cow's face. The trucks stop on the outskirts of town. We walk a short distance to Bischoffen where we are assigned to some small, three-room cottages on the edge of town that become our makeshift base for the next few days.

The job of sergeant of the guard must have been written in the stars because I am immediately given the position upon arrival. What will I be guarding this time you wonder? More loot stolen by Hitler and Hermann Göring? Goodness, Hermann, you must be the richest guy in Germany by now, sadly, at the expense of so many others. This must be my lucky day! I am guarding the entrance to what appears to be a cave or a mine. It has a narrow-gauge track used for miners' cars that were probably used to transport the loot inside. The tracks start at the edge of the road at the entrance to the mine. I place my guard in position. I am curious but decide not to enter the mine. We have no lights, and the lesson I learned in the Berchestgaden salt mine is fresh in my mind, as well as the wound that's healing on my leg.

I am standing in front of one of the salt mines. The mines were full of loot stolen from across Europe.

I'm taking no chances. Additionally, I've come

194

too far to get blown to bits by a booby trap. Near town is a train with 40x8s left on a sidetrack that we are also guarding. This train holds even more stolen loot. I don't know which country it came from, but there sure is a lot of loot here that the Nazi's plundered.

A short distance from town, a small German aircraft is parked on a makeshift gravel airstrip. Frank P. Taylor is a paratrooper from Detroit, Michigan. He and I waste no time in checking out the small plane that sits at the end of the dirt and gravel airstrip. To our surprise, it has one of the most unusual engines found in an airplane, a V8 Ford engine. I didn't know that a Ford engine was being used to power and operate an airplane.

I also notice it has a very long propeller. I find it interesting that both Ford and General Motors had operating factories in Germany using forced labor during World War II.

Here I am next to a German aircraft with a Ford engine.

195

Ford Werke employed slave laborers, although this was not required by the Nazi regime. Besides being a mortar man in the 327th, Taylor is also a trained pilot. He tells me he flew a Stinson back in the States. He walks around the plane on the airstrip giving this strange aircraft a pre-check before we load up for the flight of the day. The weather is good, a perfect day to take this plane for a ride. I prop the engine, starting the engine by rotating the propeller by hand. It instantly starts. Taylor warms the engine as I climb into the passenger's seat behind Taylor. He takes the plane up off the ground a few times and then lands it back on the strip. While he shuts it down, he says, "We must find some gasoline." The gas gauge shows empty. The search is on. Taylor says, "If we can find enough gasoline, we will fly this plane back to Auxerre, France, while the other troops ride those 40x8's." Unfortunately, we cannot beg, borrow, or steal enough gasoline to take this plane for a real ride. Sadly, we must leave this unusual airplane here.

We return to town, and I begin to get settled into my new home. The original occupants left some time ago. I only know that the people who were here have harvested their small gardens, taken the food, and all their belongings with them. Later while exploring the local mountains, I find many of these people had moved into the mountains and built hut-like homes from tree branches. They somehow managed to survive. As we are moving in, I, of course, must go exploring with another Airborne trooper. We travel less than a mile when we are surprised at the sight we see in the distance. It's hard to believe that here is a mountain farm. The land is so steep, too steep to farm, in my opinion, but these people farm it. I see they have everything to survive: honeybees, cows, wheat, apples, and many other things to stay alive and healthy. I must meet these people. We venture through the brush and orchards until we come to a very old log house. I knock on the door. Boy, life is full of surprises. A German pilot answers. He introduces himself, invites us in, and introduces me and my friend to two women who are old enough to be our mothers. This Luftwaffe pilot speaks very good English. He tells us that the house belongs to the two ladies. The women say that the house is 700 years old! They also want to know if we would have dinner with them on Wednesday. Of course! Please, what time? We are told to be here around 6 pm.

I must have had a smile from ear to ear at having an opportunity for a home-cooked meal! We thank the ladies and return to our base camp.

A lot of things are happening, but we make sure we don't miss this dinner, which turns out to be the best. The ladies are very kind and very good cooks. After dinner, the pilot, who is quite the magician, entertains us with all sorts of tricks, cards, and other magic that you can't begin to imagine. I take a second look at the old log house and decide it is very old, although I can't be sure of its age. After an enjoyable evening, we return to our base.

We get word that we are moving again, and this time I get an opportunity to ride in the German version of the 40X8 horse car. I'm standing at the tracks waiting for my train to arrive. When the train stops, I load my gear into one of the cars. It's funny to see these old cars being pulled by a nice, shiny, new locomotive. The box car is loaded with many soldiers. I'm glad we don't have to share the space with forty horses. A 2-inch by 8-inch board is fastened across the front of every door of each car to prevent anyone from falling out. Once again, the floor is covered with hay to sit and sleep on and has been sprayed with DDT. Trains were used to transport many DPs, as well as the military. DDT is used as a preventative to ensure anyone who boards the trains will, hopefully, be bug-free when they get off. The train is traveling toward France in a direction that takes me through so many places I have already been, including many of the battlefields and towns that I crawled or walked through during combat. This new locomotive takes us only a short distance to the French border. The modern locomotive is disconnected and replaced by an antique steam engine from a better day. With this new locomotive, we don't travel all that fast.

I can only imagine how slow the rest of this trip will be as we are pulled by this old steam engine. After I get settled in, I make my way up to the front and climb onto the engine, next to the engineer. It's warm and comfortable as I watch the fireman shovel coal into the fire box. The fire blazes and creates enough steam for the engine to pull us up the next steep grade. I watch the fire as it glows, the flames flickering, creating

My trooper buddies and I are loaded on a 40X8, minus the 40 horses.

shadows. The shadows look as if they are dancing across the floor of the locomotive, a hypnotizing sight. It doesn't take long for me to be off into dreamland. I doze in and out of consciousness. When I wake from my spells of sleep, there is so much light emanating from the engine that I can see some of the destruction to the railroad and the surrounding area. There are many roundhouses, mostly blown to pieces, not much more than a pile of twisted steel. By riding up here with the engineer, I understand the dangers of traveling on a war-torn railroad. After five years of war, this engineer knows what he is doing with this slow train.

The train travels slowly enough for me to hop off the locomotive and walk toward my 40x8 car and hop back on. I crawl under the board trying to not disturb these sleeping brothers of mine. I feel my way through the dark until I reach the place where I have previously placed my gear and lie down on the comfortable bed of fresh hay. The aroma is so sweet. It feels good just lying here. I wasn't expecting to fall asleep or get in any dream time; the noisy, rough riding train with the nonstop clickety-clack is enough to keep the sleepiest man awake. I try to snooze a bit anyway. I am thinking about how much more fortunate I am than all those poor people heading to concentration camps that were locked in these box cars without anything. These soldiers and I have hay for a bed, food to eat, water to drink, and fresh air to breathe.

I feel the train begin to slow down. We come to a stop. I look out of the 40X8, and to my surprise, I see the most amazing orchard, especially right now. It's a pee-tree orchard! The best outdoor bathroom money can buy with enough facilities to accommodate all these men! And what luck! This train stops right in front of its entrance! I don't know who got off the car first, but I do know every man's boots hit the ground running as they chose their tree. We all finish doing our deed and board the train again to crawl along until we stop.

It seems as if this train stops more than it moves. Off to the left near a village, maybe 30 feet away, I can see an old man pushing his wheelbarrow full of long sticks of bread. The loaves are so long the ends stick out of the wheelbarrow on both sides! I can smell that fresh bread from here. I easily jump off the box car. Getting back on could be a different story, but I'll worry about that when the time comes. As I am running, the old man hands me some loaves of bread. I pay him some francs for a few of these fresh-smelling, long loaves of bread. It's been a long time since I smelled or had a taste of fresh French bread. The bread is so fresh that I can feel the warmth of the loaves in my hands. As I run along the side of the boxcar, I throw loaves of bread into the outstretched hands of these hungry men. They are very excited to get a piece of fresh bread. I manage to jump back on the moving train without killing myself, but it was well worth it for this bread!

Hours go by until we arrive at a large platform, and the train stops. I step off the train onto a wooden platform that leads into a large, makeshift chow hall. The facility uses German prisoners for labor, and they do a good job feeding the thousands of hungry troops that are passing through here. The chow isn't too bad; it beats the K-ration and definitely the C-ration. I am amazed at the mobile canteens and their ability to feed so many men each day. They are fully equipped, and I suppose we could be fed here at any time of the day or night.

The next day we climb back onboard the train to continue our journey, stopping shortly after dark, when we stop again. This time there is another train adjacent to us that is also stopped. I inquire what is going on, only to find out that the other train is full of DPs, many of whom are in need of medical assistance. All the medics on board my train go to the other train to help. We wait for an hour or two until our medics board again, and we are on our way. Yes, even after the war, our medics have a sense of duty and an obligation to help. I am proud to be associated with them.

During this trip, I spend a lot of time with the engineer and the fireman, who is always checking the firebox and shoveling in the coal. In a way, it provides peace of mind to me. It's a place where I can be comfortable, especially after dark. Sitting here where it is warm, I am daydreaming about Kay and my family as I watch the dancing shadows trying to escape from the firebox. The time seems to move on at a fast pace. This trip finally comes to an end. We traveled 644 miles, and it took about 70 hours to do it. The train traveled slowly, but for me, the time has flown by. I give thanks to the old engineer. He got us here safely. Well, all but the one unlucky fellow, who I hear managed to fall off the train. Fortunately, he was picked up by the next locomotive. A little more beat up than the rest of us, but alive.

Chapter 19
Auxerre, France

On August 1, 1945, the 101st Airborne officially opens its CP in Auxerre, France. This is the last CP in Europe for the Screaming Eagles. It is a trying time for the troops, as well as the French people. The 101st Airborne has just left the richness of Berchtesgaden and Bischoffen, Austria, to arrive in France. France has been robbed of most of its resources over the past five years by the forces of Germany. Like many other occupied countries, most of France has been reduced to a very poor state. This is an abrupt change for the men of the 101st Airborne, although speaking for myself, this is so much better than any foxhole. The 13th Airborne arrived in France in February of 1945, giving them enough time to give the Airborne units a bad reputation. It is my understanding that they never saw a day of combat. They stayed in Auxerre, France for the duration of their deployment. The least they could have done was not soil the reputation of the Airborne here in France. The 13th Airborne were the first to be loaded on ships and sent back home to the States. As they leave, there are very few positive remarks about the American GI from the people of the cities and villages where the Eagles have to make their makeshift homes while awaiting their turn to be sent back to the United States. That could be months ahead. To add fuel to the fire, the Auxerre newspaper has printed an editorial, its commentary speaking directly to the poor conduct of the troops quartered in the towns. These troops of the Screaming Eagles aren't bad people, they're just tired and want to go home.

When President Truman gives the go-ahead to drop two atomic bombs on Japan, the war is finally brought to an end on September 2, 1945, along with our training to go fight the Japanese. With all these events happening simultaneously, the troops have now completely lost control. With the thought of home on the horizon, these men have all the reason they need to go crazy about going home. Believe me, these soldiers are almost impossible to keep under control.

The military commanders try everything imaginable to keep this restless tribe busy while they await their departure orders. They offer the men college classes, sporting activities, passes to any country except the US, and various other activities. I take full advantage of the mechanic's school one of my commanding officers, Lieutenant Skomski, starts. On numerous occasions, I disassemble a jeep engine just to assemble it again. As I work on this engine, I learn what makes it function. I try to keep my mind occupied while everyone else goes crazy all around me. I am beginning to think that nothing will settle these troops down. It seems that they spend most of their time thinking or talking about when they are going home. The troops are so out of control that we build our own barbed wire stockade in an adjoining field to try to keep all these men accounted for and out of trouble. According to the book *Rendezvous with Destiny,* within two weeks there are over 139 men locked up there. Some of the men decide to escape, and many of our NCOs and lower-ranking officers are appointed to be MPs (Military Police). In fact, so many men become MPs that the military police now far outnumber the passes that are issued.

Stockade built by GIs to hold GIs while in France.

202

AUXERRE, FRANCE

My patience is getting short, worn quite thin, as I am tired of being told that it's my responsibility to keep the troops of my platoon out of trouble. The rumor goes around that if a man escapes the stockade, the sergeant of the guard will take the escapee's place. As sergeant of my guard group, I issue my own orders. During my group's watch, I have given my troops the order to shoot any man that attempts to escape. I guess the men took me seriously. No one tries to escape, and no one gets shot. I'm glad these men understand that I mean every word.

I have been the acting platoon sergeant for months now. 1st Sergeant James A. Goble must have forgotten about the "Damned Kid." I should be at the rank of technical sergeant if I am to carry the responsibility of the platoon. The frustration among the troops really begins to show when the troops begin to understand that they are not headed home until it's their turn, and that could be awhile.

The months pass. The local people slowly warm up to us and become more friendly. We have a bi-weekly dance in town. I remember the first dance we held, only a small number of women showed up. Just a bunch of guys standing around feeling lonely. As the townspeople and the GIs get more comfortable around each other, both sides begin to be friendlier, and the dances become real dances.

GIs enjoy a dance with local women.

203

Chapter 20
The End Of The Trail

GIs boarding a ship at Le Harve, France, on their way back to the United States.

    While the men wait their turn to go home, many men turn their energy toward studying for a career in the hopes of finding work whenever they finally arrive home. Fortunately for me, I am in the next group of men scheduled to leave for the States. I will have with me one of my closest, trusted friends all the way from the days of Normandy, Ralph Avila, joining me on the trip across the ocean. He is so happy to be going back to Riverside, California. He and I dress in our Class A uniforms and go into the town of Sens, France, to have a beer and a meal to celebrate the war's end and the fact that we will be going home soon.

On November 28,1945, I begin my journey home. Up the gang plank I go, onto a ship at Le Havre, France. I stop and take one last look at the harbor. Le Harve was one of the many harbors in Hitler's Atlantic Wall which spanned the coast of Europe, all the way to Scandinavia. I think back to the time when Le Harve had been declared a Festung (fortress) by Hitler, to be held to the last man. The objective of Operation Astonia, the Allied attack on the port of Le Harve, was to secure the harbor facilities intact and to deliver supplies to the Allied armies. The Allies refused to let the civilian population be evacuated, despite offers of free passage by the fortress commander. The Royal Navy and Royal Air Force carried out a blockade and extensive preparatory bombardment of the city, which killed over 2,000 civilians and 19 German troops. The German garrison of about 11,000 men surrendered on September 12, 1944. The port was badly damaged, but it was reopened on October 9, 1944. This is the last time that my eyes will take in the destruction caused by this war, though I know the people of France will rebuild.

As I reach the deck, I notice this ship is much different than the Liberty ship that I crossed this rough ocean on two years ago. I am told the ship is an Italian luxury liner, but I personally don't see the luxury. Our beds consist of lumber for the framework. They are stacked four high, one on top of the other, about two feet apart, with a piece of canvas stretched between four pieces of wood for a mattress. The ship is crowded with men, much more crowded than my trip to Europe. I don't mind. It's not so bad because we are going home. The ship travels much faster than the slow Liberty Ship that brought me here at a snail's pace. During the trip, I have no trouble with seasickness. The ocean is calm, and I have changed my diet to vegetables. To pass the time, I usually can be found on deck, outside watching the sea life and thinking about my family, especially my mom. I also think about Kay. I never said goodbye to her, but sadly, that's how things work sometimes in war. I am also thinking about how proud I am of myself after spending the last couple of years bearing the burden of war: the victories, the moments of despair, but especially the loss of so much life. I'm fortunate I made it through all the challenges I faced. I wouldn't have had it any other way.

During the day, the sailfish entertain and amaze me as they come flying out of the water, sailing through the air with such speed, diving from one wave to another. After dark, I am back on deck watching the stars and the moon. It is so beautiful. I wonder if my mom is gazing at the stars and watching the moon as well. I am all alone, up front on the starboard side of the ship. Lonely? No, not really. I am away from the noise of the happy troops who are killing time playing cards and rolling dice. I find that this is a good place to think. The only noise is the rippling water as the ship glides peacefully through this quiet ocean. The water rises along the side of ship, and as it rolls away, it makes different colors in the moonlight. So many thoughts pass through my mind in a short time. I don't know what my future will be or if I will be able to adjust to life in this other world that I will soon be returning to. I have no money, no trade, no nothing. My only experience is the .30 caliber machine gun and trying to stay alive for the last two years. I think of Al Capone, the gangster, with his machine gun squads. I know I'm qualified for a position in an organization like that, but I am tired of the world of killing and being shot at. Yes, I'm very tired.

I made a promise to myself when I was hungry out on the battlefield that after this war ends, neither I nor any friend of mine will ever go hungry. I will do whatever it takes to survive. There must be work for a guy with my drive and determination. They say curiosity killed the cat, but I am so curious about life. I want to do everything, discover everything, and learn about everything.

There's no end to the volumes of thinking I've done about the many things that I plan to accomplish. First and most important is finishing high school, then maybe college. I like the idea of becoming a bush pilot. I want to fly my own airplane or maybe be a logger in the Northwest. Maybe I should become a big game hunter. I remember seeing all those boar mounts. Now that would bring some excitement and entertainment! Perhaps I'll go to a wild place like Alaska. I'm sure a seasoned fellow with my skills would be of use there. I have so many wonderful ideas and plans. Sadly, they always come to a halt by the same thing: money. I have no money to venture into all these dreams and no idea how or if I'll be able to earn any. I know that working in the coal mines is not the life for me. Yes, money has always been and will always be a barrier to be dealt with.

It's now time for me to visit dreamland. I have always had trouble sleeping. I never seem to get enough. I suppose it would help if I went to bed instead of staying up thinking about all my grand plans and adventures. There's just so much of life to experience and never enough time.

I am up early the next morning, ready for another adventurous day. I have a good breakfast, and then I spend some time thinking about all the complaining I did about how bad the K-and C-rations were. Then I realize that's really not how I feel. I was just blowing off steam. The vivid memory of those starved, unfortunate DPs is etched into my mind, eating maggot-filled soup, lest they starved to death. Yes, sometimes I am guilty of not being thankful enough for what I have, especially after all I have seen and experienced in my short life.

Today is the "Big Day," and as this large ship slowly maneuvers itself into the New York harbor, its cargo begins to stir. The warriors of yesterday begin bursting from its belly. The decks are quickly covered with men as we get closer to land. I'm wondering what is on each one of these men's minds. You might think there would be all sorts of hooting and hollering from all these men returning home, but instead, I notice their somber moods. Their silence takes over as the distance to home gets shorter and shorter. I'm no different. I suppose we can't believe what we see taking place. We stay quiet, but the silence is golden. I really can't explain what's going through my mind, let alone what's going on in my brothers' minds.

We are very close to having our feet touch back down on the ground in the United States. Standing here on the deck at the front of the ship, I can see the features of the Statue of Liberty, that beautiful French lady standing proudly, welcoming us home as we enter the New York Harbor. She has many nicknames, but I have always thought she needed a proper name, so I call her Joan, after Joan of Arc. They both remind me of strong women who fight for freedom. It's quite incredible how tall Joan is. At 305 feet from the ground to the top of her torch, it makes her as tall as a 22-story building. She has a 35-foot waist and weighs 225 tons. Heck, the tablet she holds is 35-feet wide, and her index finger is 8-feet long. She's a big girl! As the sun sets in the west, we move past her toward the docks. I see the gaze of the queen of the harbor, and I am in awe! This statue that represents freedom is now welcoming her freedom-fighting sons home. She is an incredible piece of art. The Statue of Liberty was a gift from the French people in 1876 commemorating the alliance of France and the United States during the American Revolution. I'm proud to be one of the soldiers to repay the favor and support them in their quest for freedom during World War II.

The Statue Of Liberty, Joan, as I like to call her.

The ship slowly pulls into the dock, and as it is being tied to the dock with giant ropes, I can't help but notice the size of the policemen patrolling the docks. Goodness, where did these gigantic fellows come from? I've never seen policemen, let alone any men, as large as these. It's as if one guy equals three! We begin to disembark, and surprisingly, it is very orderly. As I walk down the gangplank for the last time with my worldly belongings on my shoulder, I must admit that this duffle bag weighs considerably more than it did the first time I walked up the gang plank from this harbor, headed for the unknown. I take one last look at this Queen of the Harbor, Joan, the beautiful Lady Liberty, and my mind fills with thoughts of freedom. I realize that's what I am really looking for now that I have returned home.

Two years and it seems as if nothing has changed. It appears that the same 6x6 trucks that brought me here will be our transportation back to Fort Meade. A trooper keeps his eyes on me as we take our short ride to the fort. He finally says to me, "Where's home?" I tell him I am on my way south to Virginia, on the Kentucky border. His face lights up. He says that he is going to the bluegrass country of Kentucky. "I see," I say to him. "That's where you have the pretty horses and fast women." He smiles, "Right." he says, "I see we are from the same tribe." It's only then that I notice the similarity between us. Our uniforms are identical down to the shiny, brown leather boots and Eagle patches that we proudly have on our uniforms. Our duffle bags are on the floor between our legs. Oh, to be a fly on the wall! Our conversation would be quite funny by today's standards. "Whatcha got in that heavy duffle bag?" "Yours don't look very empty either." "It's only a few souvenirs for my family." "Come on now, stop kidding me!" "What do you have in that bag?" "Just some stuff." "Stuff, my butt!" "Do you think they will search my bag?" "Boy, I sure hope not. If they do, I really will get my walking papers." I quit stalling. I say to him, "I have a GI soap box full of money that I acquired from each country that I visited.

My collection of coins and bills from the seven countries I was in. This bill was signed by many of the men I shared my experiences with. Some coins date back to the 1800s.

I also have a Nazi armband with a swastika, which looks very much like the one that Hitler was always wearing. Who knows, at one time in history, he could have worn this souvenir I carry."

German swastika armband that I found in a building near a lake in Germany.

The time moves much too fast when I am sitting with good company. I ask him, "Were you up at the happy hunting ground?" He replies, "Happy hunting ground? I don't get it." "Berchtesgaden," I say. "Oh, yes, the hunting ground, happy times," he replies.

Here are some of the other souvenirs that I collected from Normandy to Berchestgaden:

German Gewehr 98 that I found in Berchestgaden. When I returned home I used this as my hunting rifle for big game like elk and bear.

German field radios I accquired in Berchestgaden. I found them in a field abandoned by German soldiers. These radios were used by the artillery and mortar men to communicate locations of potential targets.

U.S. first aid kit. This was especially interesting to me because it was made of solid brass. I'm not sure where I picked this up, but I'm glad I have it.

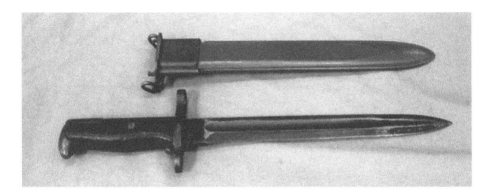

Bayonet that attaches to the infantrymen's rifle for close combat fighting. I got this item in Berchestgaden.

German combat helmet that I picked up in Normandy. The design of this helmet is smaller than the U.S. counterpart. It also has a lower profile than an American helmet. It is my understanding that many Germans had their necks broken because of the design of this helmet. Like most of the souvenirs I have, I kept it stored in my duffle bag at base camp while I was out on various missions and patrols.

Finally, this uncomfortable 6x6 comes to a halt at Fort Meade. I will never forget how comfortable those DUKWs back in the Alps were. As I offload from the truck, I'm thinking about who is going to be the happiest to be rid of me, the army here at Fort Meade, the farmer's pigs in Opheusden, Holland, or the reader who is reading my story? My mind is full and shifting from thought to thought, making it hard for me to take this all in. I am assigned to the barracks. As I begin getting settled back at Fort Meade, I see nothing here has changed. This is the army, Mr. Jones, except now, if you can imagine, I get a couple of fried eggs, over easy with ham on the side. The coffee sure hasn't gotten any better. It tastes exactly the same. I need to add a bit of cream and sugar in it to kill the bitterness before I attempt to enjoy it. Thankfully, it is much, much hotter than the K-ration recipe I have become accustomed to.

The big day is close at hand. It's time to take my finals. First, the doctor takes a look at me. I can see he is satisfied that I am alive and vertical. He thinks I'm ready to face the real world, although he doesn't check inside my head. That might have changed his mind. While getting checked out by the doctor, the POWs take my uniform and are busy sewing and getting my uniform ready for the departure, and a fine job they do! You know, these Germans are so professional at anything they take on. My uniform is returned to me in much better condition. They were pretty good on the frontlines as well, but we were better. I get dressed and await my turn to leave this place.

A couple of days go by before I board another coal burner. Avila is heading west, back to California, and I am heading south to Christiansburg, Virginia, which is near where my eldest brother, Lester, lives in Belspring. I shake hands with my friend, Avila, and promise to stay in touch. "Kentucky," the trooper I met earlier, and I board our train heading south. We reach Christiansburg, and I shake Kentucky's hand and bid him goodbye, never to see him again. He is going farther south before the tracks turn west into Kentucky.

I take a short ride in a taxi and arrive at Lester's doorstep. I'm excited to see him, his wife, Geraldine, my niece, Shirley, and nephew, Bobby, as

215

well as Geraldine's sisters. Sadly, Lester is down south near my mom and dad's home in Pound, Virginia, working in one of the coal mines. They are a lovely family. I enjoy the environment so much, especially all the pretty local girls, that I stay on for a few days. It's almost Christmas as I load my duffle bag onto the bus for the last leg of my adventurous ten-thousand-mile trip. I'm laughing to myself, wondering where the company got the name Greyhound? It should have been called, "The Weiner Dog Special," or "The Three-Legged Dog." This thing is as slow as a tortoise! Heck, it's even slower than the trains I have been on. Naturally, I just want to get home, but this bus must stop at every cow pasture along the way. The weather isn't helping our speed either. It is cold and large snowflakes are falling, threatening a deep snow.

The bus finally finds its way through this mountainous, narrow, snow-covered highway. I wake up from a deep sleep as I hear the bus driver yelling, "Pound, all off for Pound." As I get myself together and begin dragging all my worldly belongings in the duffle bag down the aisle of the bus, I can't help but think, Pound, what a strange name for a town. I flash back to my grade school days when my teacher told me a little story about the name. She said at one time this was Indian country, and there was a big field up the river a short distance. Here there is a meadow where they grazed ("pound" in Indian language)

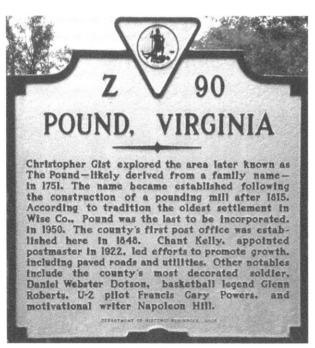

Christopher Gist explored the area later known as The Pound—likely derived from a family name—in 1751. The name became established following the construction of a pounding mill after 1815. According to tradition the oldest settlement in Wise Co., Pound was the last to be incorporated in 1950. The county's first post office was established here in 1848. Chant Kelly, appointed postmaster in 1922, led efforts to promote growth, including paved roads and utilities. Other notables include the county's most decorated soldier, Daniel Webster Dotson, basketball legend Glenn Roberts, U-2 pilot Francis Gary Powers, and motivational writer Napoleon Hill.

DEPARTMENT OF HISTORIC RESOURCES, 2006

Historical marker was erected in 2006, by Department of Historic Resources. It is located at the bridge over Indian Creek.

their horses, but we know also that most of these Native Americans walked. The name most likely came from the pounding mill that was opened in 1815. Pound, or "the Pound" as it is known, was established after the construction of the mill. Also, this was Daniel Boone's hunting ground. When I was twelve, maybe a little older, my grandad and

In the early 1930s, the Daniel Boone tree was struck by lightning. Because of its popularity, the Louisville, KY community wanted to save the tree, but a tree surgeon declared the tree 99% dead. It was then decided to try to save the inscription portion of the tree. In April 1932, a four-foot section with the inscription was removed and given to the Filson Club, now the Filson Historical Society, for preservation.

I traveled to a place he referred to as the "Breaks of the Mountain, The Grand Canyon of the South." I hear there is a tree that stands near there with the carving "D. Boone kilt a bar." That was around the year 1760. As I step off the bus a stranger moves toward me. "Hi, soldier, what could be your name? I am McKinley Steel." I reply, "I am George Mullins." "Who is your dad?" I say, "Bill Mullins." He replies, "I am a son of a gun!

I know him. In fact, he's a distant kin of mine. Do you have a ride?" "No, I am footing it." "Would you like me to give you a ride? I know where your dad lives. It's only twelve miles on the South Fork." I take Mr. Steel up on his offer and avoid another walk in the cold. I think I have had enough of that for a bit. We walk to Steel's truck and get in. I see Steel is a good driver, as we move along slowly in his old truck, taking his time in this bad weather. We are within a mile of where I grew up. Steel and I have to park here and walk across a small, snow-covered bridge. The moon is shining brightly, and the reflection on the fresh snow lights up the path enough that we do not need a flashlight. I am proud of my strength. I am carrying the heavy duffle bag and walking through the snow with Steel. The big mountaineer is having a hard time keeping up with me. We reach the house, walk up the short steps, and knock on the door. I hear my mom's voice say, "Come in." I open the door and step into the living room. The element of surprise must have walked in before me. There is silence for a couple of seconds. My family is shocked, speechless, as I stand there. I have my eyes on my mom. I know she can't believe what she is seeing. No, Mom, it's really me, not a ghost. It is your Georgie. Suddenly, it's like a bomb hit the living room. My mom grabs me as my dad jumps out of bed, yelling and dancing with my little brothers and sisters. They were all so startled they did not know what to do. The sad part of this reunion is my dad is not well. With all this commotion, his energy is quickly spent. I know he wants to stay up and visit, but he must return to bed because he is very sick. My oldest brother, Lester, is here. He is in bed sick as well.

The chaos of the situation caused by my arrival has begun to settle a bit; the shock of my being home is joyfully and quickly accepted. I guess it is fair play that the element of surprise is repaid to me. My mom moves towards me and says in a low voice, "I have a Christmas present for you." She hands me a little package wrapped in a blanket. Oh, the suspense! I wish not to keep you waiting! It must be one of those military secrets that I have heard so much about. Gently, I remove the cover. I am blinking my eyes to clear them. When they do clear, I see a brand-new little baby, my sister, Patty. If the element of surprise ever worked in my life, it did its job this time. I am completely speechless. Sorry, no baby picture but this is

My baby sister, Patty.

what happened to this little bundle of love as she got older.

Mr. Steel, who has been completely forgotten about, is eager to be on his way. I walk with him back to his vehicle and thank him for his help. I then hurry back home. With all the excitement and surprises, I'm trying to bury what I have become used to. My mind is full, and I get very little sleep that night. I am up early the next morning. After enjoying a fresh cup of mom's coffee, I know what I must do. I am out the door, take Lester's car, and am on my way to get the country doctor. The doctor comes back to the house with me. After his examination of my dad and brother, he reveals that my brother has pneumonia, and my dad has double pneumonia! The doctor asks me, "George, can you give a shot?" I reply, "I gave a few morphine shots during the war." He says, "That's good enough. You give your brother and dad one shot every two hours. Have your family wake you and don't miss giving either of them their shot. As long as they get them, I am sure they will be okay."

The doctor and I leave the house, get into the car, and have an enjoyable ride back to his office in town. I pay him for his services and let him know how much I appreciate him. I return home to find my two patients already on the mend.

Another surprise is waiting for me, another Christmas present! My brother, Vernoy, who is an MP, military police, stationed in Florida, has

Happy times! My brother, Vernoy, and I, Christmas 1945.

THE END OF THE TRAIL

arrived at our family home. Hopefully, he can keep me out of trouble this Christmas season! He has an amazing smile and a jolly personality. I am glad he's here.

My dad and brother are both on the mend. During these happy times, I have a nagging voice in the back of my mind. I have been gone for a bit, two years, two months, and eleven days, and now that I'm back, I find things haven't changed very much in these mountains. The depression and its effects have lingered, even after all my time away. Most people have not come close to recovering. Jobs pay more, but with the war over, layoffs are in abundance. Since I returned, I find myself in the same situation I was in before I left. I look at all the options I have available, and sadly, my common sense tells me I can't buy a job, let alone find someone to hire me at a livable wage.

In the early spring of 1946, my family and I move to Blacksburg, Virginia, hoping to find work. This also allows me to register at Blacksburg High School to finish my schooling. My family struggles, as there are no jobs here, but we get by. The powder plant twenty-five miles away in Radford, Virginia, has also closed, so there is no hope for a job there.

During the war, jobs became plentiful because so many items were needed to support the war effort. From coast to coast, millions of men and women worked in war industries. The workers were proud to be part of the effort. Thirty-five percent of the workforce were women, and all workers felt like they were doing their part. It was better than the prewar economy when a full day's work was only paying one dollar. During the war, wages were better, around eight dollars a day. However, the increase in jobs and wages didn't reach the mountains of Western Virginia.

While I was away, I heard many suggestions, stupid opinions, recommendations, and plans so grand it would leave you speechless about what a person should do or was going to do upon return. I don't see many opportunities for me living here in rural Virginia. I left here broke with only the clothes on my back. I find upon my return home that nothing has changed, my life is the same, I have only the clothes on my back, and

I wouldn't have those except that Uncle Sam gave them to me. There are no trade jobs for an expert machine gunner. All my worldly experience to date is useless for what few jobs are here near home. I don't know what my future holds, but I know there has to be work for me somewhere. I know that I'll find something.

One thing I have available since I came home is time to think. I spend some time trying to bury the events of war that haunt my mind. I think about Germany and the crazy man who wanted to conquer the world. Hitler was well on his way to accomplishing his dream of 1000 years of world domination and might have achieved it had it not been for our intervention. His success was short-lived, only twelve years. It is my sincere hope that when Europeans think about freedom; they will always remember that America was there for that reason: freedom.

The reassurance the U.S. soldier provided during the war is something that cannot be taken lightly. He was a sign of hope that there was a chance that everything would turn out okay and fortunately for me and many others, it did. I think about all the men and women who didn't survive; their lives taken too soon, robbed of the gift of life by a crazy man, as well as the DPs who will never return to the lives they once had. I also think about that part of the German military and the people of Germany who have to live out their lives knowing they supported or were complacent about Hitler and his policies. Freedom reigns supreme, and I am thankful for the many Germans who sacrificed their lives in the fight against tyranny. They are all unspoken heroes. Mostly, I am thankful for all the prayers my mom said while I was away. I truly believe that it was her thoughts and prayers that safely guided me on my journey until I returned home. My hopes and my dreams are that an event as terrible as this one was will remain in every human's mind, and that the atrocities of war will serve as a reminder to never let history repeat itself.

Chapter 21
My Post-War Life

I know that my story is written in the stars, but I hope that some of my dreams are included in that story. Yes, dreams do come true.

I finish two years of high school in one year and graduate in June 1947. When I finish school, I begin to get restless. My curious mind and adventurous soul calls me to the Pacific Northwest.

My first dream complete. I graduated from high school in Blacksburg, Virginia, in June of 1947.

My brother, Vernoy and I travel in an old 1936 Pontiac. As we travel, I take note of the differences between the United States and Europe. The biggest difference is that no place in the United States shows any sign of war. I have seen so much death and destruction in the past couple of years that to see this beautiful, untouched land makes me thankful to be living in America.

I reach Raymond, Washington, in July 1947. I take a job as a lumberjack in an amazing jungle of all types of trees. The land is full of wild game, lakes and rivers with many fish, and oysters and clams in the bays.

I try to stay in contact with my beautiful Kay, but as the months pass, it seems as if the time in-between letters get farther apart. Kay finally sends me a letter letting me know she has found another, an RAF pilot, and they will be married soon. It hurts a bit, but I understand and can't say I blame her. I never told her the reason I didn't bring her back to the States with me at the end of the war, but I wish I had. It wouldn't have mattered to her, but it did to me. I really cared for her. I also knew I had nothing to offer this young woman. No job or home, only me. As time has passed, I have come to realize that was all she wanted: me. Not what I had or didn't have, just me. Sadly, in those days, I didn't understand what is the real wealth in life. It's not mansions, limousines, or jewels; the real wealth in life is love! To love and be loved is truly the meaning of happiness for me.

I was discharged from the reserves in early 1948. Because the level of the military forces had fallen below the necessary numbers, President Truman decided to reinstate the draft for men between the ages of 19 and 26 years old in July that same year. I fell right into that category but felt safe as I had already served my time.

1949 was a difficult year for me. I re-enlisted in the Army reserves in March of that year. In August, I got married for the first time. A couple of months later, I was involved in a work-related accident. As a logger, I knew the dangers of working in the woods, but I never expected what was about to happen. I was busy pulling a cable to move a log. Up the mountain above me, a log broke free and rolled down the hill, crushing my leg between the two massive logs. It broke my leg in numerous places. I still have a metal plate and seven screws in my leg that hold it all together.

After getting hurt, things seemed to go from bad to worse. I couldn't work with my leg all busted up. The Korean War started in June of 1950. I was called back to active duty and found myself once again in an army uniform. I was happy to stay in the U.S. this time. I was assigned to the Army Security Agency Training Center and School (ASA) at the Carlisle Barracks in Pennsylvania as a motor pool sergeant at the training center, although my job entailed more than just the motor pool. I also securely destroyed classified information for the army.

My second round in the Army.

My daughter, Sheila, was born in the hospital at the Carlisle Barracks on February 19, 1951. We moved the ASA to Fort Devens in Massachusetts a couple months after she was born. I returned to Washington in the winter of 1951 where I finally was discharged from the military for good, I am forever thankful that Korea was not part of my story. I went back to Virginia in April 1952 to gather up and help the rest of my family migrate to the West Coast. In 1957, I moved to California and never looked back.

My daughter, Sheila, and I at Fort Devens, Massachusetts.

225

I have been blessed in this life. I have made and been given so much opportunity to do and experience so many of my dreams. Yes, dreams do come true. These are some photos of my family and a few of the many work experiences I have been fortunate to have after returning home:

Cold deck with heel boom used in the early logging days. The heel boom lifted the logs onto trucks or train beds. I had one of these logs roll from the deck and crush my leg.

I became a lumberjack, another dream complete. My dad stands on the stump of a giant Redwood tree that I had just felled outside of Redway, California.

Here I am in my Tri-Champ. My son, Doug, and his friend are in the backseat.

Another dream comes true. I landed a 1940 N3N Navy trainer biplane in Garberville, California.

I spent some time working as a fisherman, part of the Mosquito Fleet in Northern California. This is my boat, Lucy of Shelter Cove, named after my wife.

King salmon fishing at its finest!

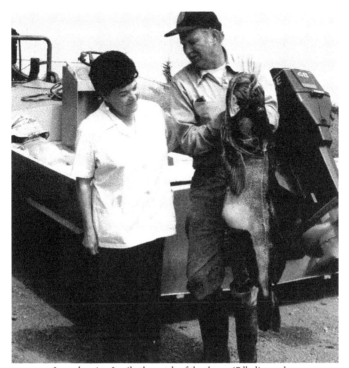

I am showing Lucila the catch of the day, a 47 lb. lingcod.

My son, Greg, and I halibut fishing in Alaska.

My first construction truck. It was an old army 6X6 with a cement mixer attached to it. I poured a lot of cement with this truck!

Another hot day digging a trench in beautiful Northern California.

My first backhoe. I got it in 1965 after the Christmas flood of 1964 that was so devastating to Humboldt County and Northern California that it was deemed a thousand-year flood.

Doing trench work on the side of a hill with my 21-ton excavator.

My first wife with my children. Taken in Redway, CA circa 1966.
Back Row: Mark, Ina Jean (my 1st wife), and Sheila.
Front Row: Doug, Philip, and Greg.

Lucila and I with all our children circa 1980.
Back Row: Beto, Martha, Rick, Lucila, George, Sheila, Mark, and Greg.
Front Row: Yolanda, Toby, Philip, and Doug.

My siblings and I all grown up.
Front: Bill and Minnie, my dad and mom.
Center: Ozie, Mable, Dicie, and Patty, my beautiful sisters.
Back: Lester, George, Vernoy, Orbie, Harlis, Harold, and Hillard, my brothers and I.

Lucila and I on our wedding day, August 12, 1978.

If I had my life to do over again, I'd find you sooner so I could love you longer.

Lucila's daughter, Yolanda, and I at Lucila's gravesite in May 2016.

In Loving memory of Lucila Mullins

Epilogue 1
Trips Back To Europe

I have been fortunate over the last 26 years to return many times to the places where I fought and celebrate with the locals who truly appreciate their freedom. Each visit I make reignites the memories of all the men I shared these experiences with. Here are some photos from my visits back to the seven countries I hold so dear:

Ticker tape parade in Holland. Courtesy of the Best Defense Foundation.

This ID badge was given to me on my first trip back to Europe for the 50th anniversary of the invasion of Normandy.

Lucila and I with Séverine Kairis in Bastogne. Severine was only 12 at the time, but she, her family, and I are still dear friends to this day.

TRIPS BACK TO EUROPE
September 2004

Dear Veteran,

I'm writing to say " Thank You ", and, through me, there are thousands of children speaking to thousands of Veterans.

Like us, you were young and carefree, but, when you were only twenty years old, Liberty called - called you, to say :

" I'm dying. Come and save me ! "

And you arose, full of courage and zeal, to answer that call.

You underwent training, day after day, for "D" Day, and, one day in June, you arrived by air and sea.

And you fought with the heart and soul of a free man, so that we, too, might be free.

You saw your fellows fall on our beaches and in our fields and, in spite of your grief and your injuries, you stayed on and fought side-by-side with us.

And so, dear Veteran, I want to tell you, regarding those dear to you who sacrificed their youth and are now resting in peace, the sleep of the just, that,

WE ARE THE CHILDREN THEY NEVER HAD.

And to you, dear Veteran, who offered your bravery and your most promising years for this our land, I say to you,

WE ARE YOUR SONS, SONS AND DAUGHTERS OF LIBERTY, who want to say to you today, a heartfelt "THANK YOU ! "

Jean

This postcard was given to me during the celebration of the 60th anniversary of the liberation of Holland. Poem text by Jean Goujon. Facebook page: "les Chemins de la Liberté" by Jean Goujon.

Arriving for the 60th anniversary celebration of the liberation of Holland, my daughter, Sheila, son-in-law, Don, and I were met at the airport by Jan Vrenssen, our host from the Society of Dutch Airborne Friends. From this first meeting on September 13, 2004, we were treated like royalty by the Dutch during our stay, and Jan became one of our dearest friends.

In 2004, while visiting Holland with my daughter, Sheila, I came upon a group of schoolchildren and their teachers who had ridden their bikes to this memorial dedicated to the 101st Airborne. I was thrilled to have the opportunity to speak with them.

Standing at one of the Market Garden memorials dedicated to the 101st Airborne in Holland.

TRIPS BACK TO EUROPE
September 2004

8,301 of our military heroes rest in the beautiful Netherland American Cemetery and Memorial in Margrateen, their headstones set in long curves.

I met this grateful woman in 2004 at Bois de la Paix, the Peace Woods, located in Bastogne, Belgium. Her sign and smile say it all.

September 2004

A television reporter interviews me about my experiences during the Battle of the Bulge as we stand at the Mardasson Memorial, a monument honoring the memory of American soldiers wounded or killed during the battle.

I was happy to see a replica under construction of the Waco CG-4A glider that carried me into Holland at the Wings of Liberation Museum in Best, Holland.

June 2017

I had the pleasure of receiving the keys to the city of Carentan, France, from the mayor, Jean-Pierre Lhonneur. Below is the medal I was also awarded in Carentan.

I was honored to receive the French Legion of Honor (Légion d'Honneur) while in Carentan, France, in June, 2017 from the Préfet de la Manche, Mr. Jean Marc Sabathé. A préfet is the local representative for the French president. This award, the highest decoration bestowed in France, was established in 1802 by Napoleon Bonaparte.

This bench, located in front of the Kyriad Hotel in Carentan, France was commissioned by the hotel's owner, my dear friend Anne-Lyse Johnson and her husband, Peter Johnson. A large beam was salvaged from a bombed and destroyed castle in Auxais, France, and a bench was made in my honor. There is a bullet hole in the bench from the war.

June 2017

I am kneeling beside the birch tree and plaque dedicated to me in the Bois de la Paix, the Wood of Peace, in Bastogne. During the 50th anniversary of the Battle of the Bulge, 4,000 trees were planted, honoring the Allied and Belgium combatants who fought for freedom. It is laid out to recreate the UNICEF emblem: a mother and child, symbol of human tenderness. This design is only visible from the air.

247

70 years later, I am back in Normandy near where I landed on Utah Beach. Yes, I can still pack a machine gun with the best!

TRIPS BACK TO EUROPE
June 2018

Standing against the first wall I saw in Carentan. This wall and location hold many memories; some good, some not so good, of my time here 74 years ago. Courtesy of Best Defense Foundation.

Placing a flag on Omaha beach with a young French girl. The children in France and Europe have a much different view of veterans, especially from World War II. Courtesy of Best Defense Foundation.

249

Members of the Best Defense Foundation and I in Normandy at the Le Monte-Saint-Michel castle in the tidewater. This castle was built around 900 A.D. The BDF made my most recent trips possible, bringing me back to all these wonderful places, as well as providing me with photos from these trips. Special thanks to Magali Desquesne, owner of DDay4you Tours, for showing us this special place.

Left to right: David Poulain, Magali Desquesne, Kathryn Edwards, Madisson Solid, Ronald "Rondo" Scharfe, Anna Becker, Donnie Edwards, Bilal "Bibi" Mustphaoul, Gwenael Jacob, Michael Malone, Aaron Turkel, Andre Chappaz, Ralph Peters, Austin Bishop, Joe Conway, Liberty Phillips, Patrick McCue, and me.

I never danced at our dances in Auxerre, France. 73 years later, I finally got a French woman to dance with me!

USO (United Service Organizations) at its finest!

TRIPS BACK TO EUROPE
June 2018

Three Airborne troopers stand with Anje Van Buuren as she shares her story during our final day in Holland. She was just a six-year-old child when Operation Market Garden began on September 17, 1944. Right before her eyes, she saw the paratroopers jumping out of airplanes with their white parachutes, like angels falling from the sky. Courtesy of Best Defense Foundation.

I had the pleasure of meeting my dear friend, artist and poet Karen Bauer, her husband, Rene, and her son, Max, in Holland. Karen wrote the beautiful poems in my book.

74 years later, I returned to Berchestgaden. I'm standing on the steps leading to the Big House. I walked up and down these stairs to the mess hall every day while I was part of the occupation force. Courtesy of Best Defense Foundation.

Tom Rice and I are in the long tunnel leading to the gleaming brass elevator that ascends 406 feet to the Eagle's Nest. This mountain top chalet, completed in 1938, sits at an elevation of over 6,000 feet and was used by members of the Nazi Party for government and social events.

TRIPS BACK TO EUROPE
June 2019

Tom Rice and I are standing in the main reception room of the Eagle's Nest in front of a fireplace of red Italian marble, a gift from Benito Mussolini, which was damaged by Allied soldiers chipping off pieces to take home as souvenirs. One of these pieces was returned and glued back in.

I am in La Fiere, France, near the La Fierge bridge over the Merderet River, where elements of the 82nd Airborne landed on D-Day, seeing the sight as it looked then: angels of liberation falling from the sky.

The first time I went to Europe in 1944, I was an 18-year-old kid fighting a war. Here I am in 2019 at 94, back in Europe with the descendants of those I helped liberate.

Epilogue 2
The Men of 1st Battalion, Company C, 327th GIR, 101st Airborne

There are so many men I must give my thanks to. Without them, I might not be here to tell this story or at least, the story as I see it. My friend, Julius Meade, returned to the States about the same time as I did. He was part of the 5th Armored Division, as well as the 46th Armed Infantry. He married and raised his family in Pound, Virginia. He passed away on May 22, 2014. Edward Shortt was KIA on November 19, 1944. He was a great soldier and a dear friend. To this day, I think about him.

I never saw Stanley Skomski again, but he is responsible for my knowledge of mechanics. Without his instruction and education, I would know nothing about engines and their inner workings. It is my understanding that Randol Patey was KIA back in Normandy from sniper fire. James Gobles started a jump school after the war in Kansas. I was fortunate to spend some time with him in his home. Ralph Avila returned to Riverside, California, where he became a mason. I was fortunate to find him after the war, but he passed away shortly after we reconnected. Kenneth Whalen became 1st Sergeant of C Company, 327th GIR. He was a good man, as well as a great sergeant and friend. I didn't mention this before, but his nickname was Sergeant Snuffy, although none of us had the guts to call him that to his face. He was KIA in North Korea, along with many other men on September 26, 1950. Captain Walter H. Miller went on to help write the book *Rendezvous with Destiny*. He reached the rank of lieutenant colonel before retiring, and he became the secretary-treasurer of the 101st Airborne Division Association. Without him, I might have been buried alive by one of our own Sherman tanks. Chaplain Crosby retired from the military and became a minister at a church in Alexandria, Virginia. I am forever grateful for the letter he wrote to my mom. To this day, it is one of my prized possessions. My big brother and dearest of friends, Herschel Parker, went to Korea and became a master sergeant. When he retired, he went back to Dallas, Texas and became a barber. He and I remained close until he passed away in the early 1980s. I will always hold him in the highest respect. I never saw Carl Ewell again.

Parker told me years later that he also returned to Dallas, but I never reconnected with him after the war. I don't know what happened to Lieutenant Carlock. I never saw him again, but he remains in my mind today. He was nothing like the other officers. In fact, even he used to agree he was too much like the enlisted men and would never be promoted to the higher ranks. I was fortunate enough to visit with Joseph Henn a couple of times in Petersburg, Nebraska. I will always remember the wonderful pheasant dinner I shared with him. I remember the sour look on all the faces of the men as Donald Scott loaded up his jeep with that five gallons of schnapps. There are so many men who are a part of this story. I wish I knew all their names. They were all freedom fighters and deserve our respect.

This is a list of the men who served with me in the 1st Battalion, Company C, 327th GIR, 101st Airborne. I cannot guarantee the completeness of the roster, but wanted credit given to all the men who were a part of the 101st Airborne 327th GIR. It does not reflect final ranks of each individual, but their rank as of the creation date of the roster, or actual known rank. To me, they all are unsung heroes.

Pfc. Paul L. Abbey
Pvt. Paul Abel
Sgt. Willis E. Adams
　　　Joseph L. Adducci
Pfc. John Albani
Cpl. William E. Allen
Pvt. Leighton O. Allison
Pfc. Ray W. Anderson
Pfc. Delbert K. Anderson
　　　Floyd Anderson
Sgt. Thomas L. Anglin
　　　Victor Appel
1st Lt. Quentin Armstrong
Pfc. Walter A. Ashorn
Pfc. Ralph R. Avila
Pfc. Robert J. Baillargeon
Pfc. Cosmo A. Barberi
Pfc. Edwin M. Baron
　　　James E. Bear
　　　Robert Bear
　　　M. W. Beightol
Pfc. Sherman J. Bird
Pfc. Charles R. Bixler
Pfc. Albert Boggs
1st Lt. Clifford J. Bollander Jr.
Pfc. Willis J. Bovenschen
2nd Lt. William W. Boyles
Sgt. John Brechko
　　　Earnest Brickell
1st Lt. Harold W. Brown
Ssgt. Emmanuel Brunner
Pvt. Clarence L. Bullion

Pfc. Charles W. Burgess
　　　Llewellyn V. Burrows
　　　Ora D. Butcher
Pfc. Otis B. Cady
Pfc. Tony J. Calabrese
　　　Robert W. Campbell
1st Lt. Robert H. Carlock
Pvt. Joseph L. Carpenter
1st Lt. Francis L. Champoux
2nd Lt. Peter J. Chapon
Ssgt. Harold T. Chappell
　　　Gerold Chappell
　　　Frank Churchill
Sgt. Thomas M. Clark
2nd Lt. Curtis H. Clay
Pfc. Warren P. Clemen
　　　Lloyd R. Clinkingbeard
Pfc. Maysel H. Coe
　　　Roger Cole
Pfc. Jack D. Collins
Pvt. Cecil L. Conners
　　　Sidney Cordes
Pvt. Joseph W. Costagine
　　　Joseph M. Costabile
Pfc. Harry E. Cotterman
Sgt. Glen D. Cowan
Ssgt. Stu Cowen
Pvt. Earl D. Cox
　　　Langston W. Craig
Chaplin Newton G. Crosby
Ssgt. Earnest R. Cummings
Pvt. Arthur S. Cunningham
　　　John M. Cutrone

Pvt. Raymond T. Daly
Ben Darrel
Sgt. Leo D. Davis
Pfc. Eugene Davis
Leon Decker Diebel
Cpl. Anibal Delgado
Bennie K. Derrough
Pfc. Frank J. Derynioski
Ssgt. Kenneth D. DeWitt
Pvt. Edward Dietz
Pfc. Paul G. Diuble
J. Drinoski
Tech 5 Joseph P. Eberst
1st Lt. Everett D. Elliason
Patrick Enwright
Pfc. Milton I. Erlick
Sgt. Carl E. Ewell
Ssgt. Theodore Feldman
Gerald Fernholz
Pvt. William D. Fetzer
Clayton P. Flemming
Ssgt. Dale H. Fleming
Capt. Robert E. Gailbraith
Pvt. Raoul P. Garcia
Clifford D. Gardner
Tech Sgt. George Gifford
Pfc. Raymond R. Gilbert
1st Sgt. James A. Goble
1st Lt. Warren Goemaere
Pvt. Edward S. Goonan
Stanley Gorski
Ssgt. Elmer M. Grant
Victor C. Graper
Pvt. Howard Gregory
Ssgt. Jesse Griggs
Pfc. Truman Harris
Pvt. Perry R. Harwoth

Ssgt. Donald H. Hastings
Pfc. Lawrence J. Hauser
Perry R. Haworth
Robert Helden
Pfc. James R. Helmar
Pfc. Joseph M. Henn
Pfc. Richard G. Henn
Cpl. Jack M. Henn
Sgt. Ray W. Herron
1st Lt. Charles Y. Heuser
Willie Hicks
Pvt. Henry J. Hoban
Pvt. Joseph L. Hoffman
Robert F. Holden
Pvt. Robert E.L. Horton
Theodore Hotnaday
Walter M. Howard
A. E. Humphries
Ssgt. Wayne W. Huse
Pfc. Van Z. Janaway Jr.
Ssgt. Lester H. Jensen
Ssgt. William B. John
Pfc. Joseph E. Johnson
Pfc. Robert E. Johnston
Pvt. Robert C. Jones
Bill R. Jones
Pfc. Werner W. Jutzen
Pfc. Walter G. Kaelin
Pvt. Alex Kanyok
Ssgt. Melvin Keen
Pfc. Aubery Keenan
Pfc. Vivian C. Kelley
Pfc. George M. Kempf
Pfc. Charles W. Kempf
Pfc. Robert F. Kennedy
Pfc. Walter F. Knoll
Sgt. Archie P. Kobis

Pvt. Joseph J. Kulwanowski
1st Lt. Harold R. Labrie
Pfc. Harold J. Lamoen
Pvt. James T. Landrum
Pfc. Donald D. Lange
Pfc. Delmar J. Larson
Cpl. Alphonse J. Laudel
    Herbert T. Lawhorn
Pfc. Henry L. Lederman
Pfc. William H. Lemaster
2nd Lt. George M. Lovett
    George Luehring
1st Lt. Benjamin J. Luhring
Ssgt. Lester F. Lutes
Pfc. James F. Lynn
Pvt. Edward J. Lyskawa
Pfc. James W. MacMahon
Tech 5 Robert E. Mantle
Pfc. Anthony J. Maricevich
    Carl Marsh
    T.R. Martin
Pfc. William O. McClary
    Spurgeon H. McCleary
Pvt. Alexander J. McLaryety
Tech 5 Carlos Meek
Sgt. Donald M. Merrill
Pfc. Lawrence A. Michaelis
Pvt. John M. Miller
Capt. Walter L. Miller Jr.
Pvt. Afton Mills
Pfc. William Miraglio
Pvt. Andrew C. Miro
Sgt. Glen E. Moats
Pfc. John J. Molfetto
Pvt. Orville E. Monson
Pfc. David F. Moore

Pvt. Edwin M. Morgan
Pfc. Austin T. Mullenix
Ssgt. George K. Mullins
Pfc. William G. Mullins
    Edward J. Myszel
Pvt. Alex Nassavage
Capt. George Nichols
Pvt. John J. Noe
Pvt. Merlin D. Normand
    L.T. Odom
Ssgt. Robert P. Olson
Pfc. William W. Onstott
    August Orleansky
    Fernando Ortiz
Pfc. August Paolino
Ssgt. Herschel C. Parker
Pvt. George G. Parks
Pvt. Biaggio A. Passarelli
1st Lt. Randell Patey
Pfc. Earle F. Pelton
    Martin Perillo
    Mathis Perin
Pfc. Albert R. Perreault
Pvt. Gerold O. Pfeiffer
    T.J. Phillips
Pvt. Andrew P. Pilledggie
Pvt. Ralph M. Poloian
Pfc. William C. Posey
Pfc. Donald C. Price
Pfc. John S. Proctor
Pfc. Robert W. Quick
    Leonard T. Quinn
Pfc. James L. Ragan
    Donald J. Rich
Pfc. Frank Richardson
Pfc. Anthony B. Richgels

Robert B. Rider
Milton Rife
Alfred Riley
Sgt. Robert D. Risley
Pfc. Raymond A. Rodriguez
Johnny M. Rogers
Louis Rolls
Richard Rowan
Pvt. Walter C. Rupp
Sgt. Joseph S. Rusinyak
Pvt. Wesley Sachuk
Pfc. Guy E. Sakunders Jr.
Pvt. Saragosa S. Salazar
Major Hartford Salee
Sgt. Charles Salrin
Pfc. Joseph M. Satalin
Pfc. Guy E. Saunders Jr.
2nd Lt. Ralph W. Saunders
Tom Savage
Donald Scheneckenberger
Pfc. Frank C. Schircel
1st Lt. Donald C. Scott
1st Lt. Howard M. Scott
James C. Shackelford
Tech Sgt. Irving A. Sheehy
D.A. Sheptenko
Ssgt. Louis A. Sherman
Pvt. Joe Shevitz
Pfc. Herbert L. Sibole
Pvt. Jack Skinner
1st Lt. Stanley T. Skomiski
Allen E. Smithey
Pvt. Snellman
Kenton D. Snook
Pvt. Ray W. Soderquist

Pfc. Edward Stephany
Pfc. Frank D. Stkagg
Pvt. Deward Strunkle
Pvt. Stulp
Sgt. Frank Stumble Jr.
O.D. Sullivan
Pfc. Ray Swanson
Sgt. Wallace S. Swartzbaugh
Frank Szumski
Pfc. Leslie Tabler
Louis Tables
Dave Taylor
Sgt. Frank Taylor
Pfc. Andrew C. Thieneman
Pfc. Ralph E. Thomas
Pfc. Robert D. Thomas
Van C. Thomas
Sgt. Frank Thompson
Capt. Preston R. Towns
Pfc. Frank A. Tracy
Pvt. Joseph R. Trappasse
Tech Sgt. Glenn S. Travis
2nd Lt. John Turner
Sgt. Lee E. Updyke
Pfc. Carl H. Utegg
1st. Lt. William Vahue
Sgt. Joe Valsi
Ray A. Vick
Jack Vitale
Robert Vondron
1st Lt. Earnest G. Walker
Vernon Wallace-Ward
Pfc. John G. Water
Robert J. Watts
Sgt. Willie H. Webster

THE MEN OF 1st BATTALION, COMPANY C, 327th GIR, 101st AIRBORNE

1st Sgt. Kenneth J. Whalen
Pvt. John G. Weyer
    Oliver Willhite
Pfc. Eugene E. Williams
Tech Sgt. Frank B. Wilson
Sgt. Lee W. Wilson
Pfc. Frank C. Wilson
    Paul Wise
    Gordon W. Witt
    John Wojcik
    Felix J. Wojt
Pvt. Bennie J. Word
Pfc. Charles D. Yocum
    Andrew Young
    Michael Zanborsky
    Michael J. Zvosec

About the Author

George Mullins, a 96-year-old veteran and entrepreneur, brings us the story that has been living inside him since World War II. He has made many trips back to Europe, making friends everywhere he goes and has become a "rock star" to young people all over the world who are interested in World War II. From lumberjack to construction company owner and private pilot to author, George still lives by the words he always said to his 5 children, "You have to learn something every day."

The author lives in Northern California with his dog, Captain, and is looking forward to his next adventure.